RUDYARD KIPLING
IN VERMONT

Birthplace of The Jungle Books

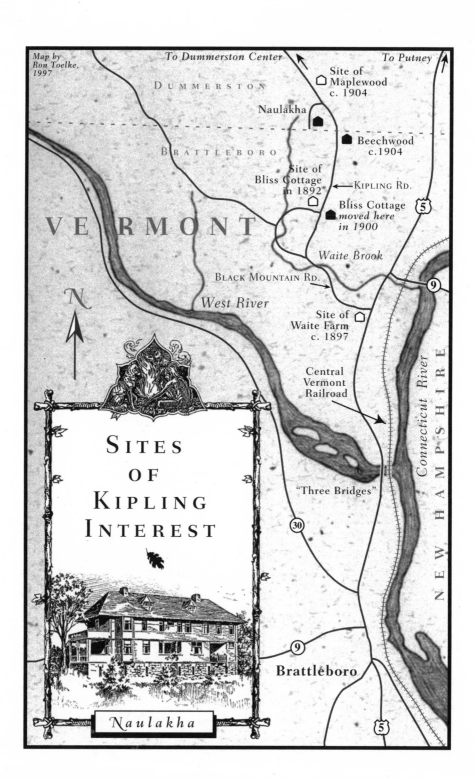

To Dummerston Center

To Putney

DUMMERSTON

Site of
Maplewood
c. 1904

Naulakha

Beechwood
c.1904

BRATTLEBORO

Site of
Bliss Cottage
in 1892

KIPLING RD.

Bliss Cottage
*moved here
in 1900*

VERMONT

Waite Brook

BLACK MOUNTAIN RD.

West River

Site of
Waite Farm
c. 1897

5

9

N

Central
Vermont
Railroad

Connecticut River

SITES

OF

KIPLING

INTEREST

"Three Bridges"

NEW HAMPSHIRE

30

9

Brattleboro

Naulakha

5

RUDYARD KIPLING IN VERMONT

Birthplace of The Jungle Books

STUART MURRAY

Images from the Past
Bennington, Vermont
by arrangement with
The Centinel Company
Hanover, New Hampshire

Cover: A view of Naulakha from the south end, showing the porch and walled garden in front of Kipling's study on the first floor; the children's nursery is directly upstairs. Inset: Kipling in his study at Naulakha in 1895.

1 2 3 4 5 6 7 8 9 10 XXX 03 02 01 00 99 99 98 97

Library of Congress Cataloging-in-Publication Data
Murray, Stuart, 1948–
    Rudyard Kipling in Vermont: birthplace of the jungle books/by Stuart Murray.
        p.   cm.
    Includes bibliographical references and index.
    ISBN 1-884592-04-X (hardcover). – ISBN 1-884592-05-8 (pbk.)
    1. Kipling, Rudyard, 1865-1936 – Journeys – Vermont..   2. Kipling, Rudyard, 1865-1936.   Jungle books.   3. Authors, English – 19th century – Biography.   4. British – Vermont – Biography.   I. Title.
PR4856.M85   1997
828' .803 – dc21
[B]   97-18692
                                                                                              CIP

Copyright© 1997 Stuart Murray
Published by Images from the Past, Inc., Bennington, Vermont 05201
Tordis Ilg Isselhardt, Publisher

Printed in the United States of America

Text and Display: Adobe Garamond
Paper: 55lb. Glatfelter Supple Opaque Recycled Natural
Cover: 12pt C1S
Composition: Macintosh 8100/80, with 172mb RAM, Quark XPress 3.32, Adobe Photoshop 3.0, Adobe Illustrator 5.5
Production: Open Prepress Interface between Stillwater Studio, Stillwater NY, and Thomson-Shore, Inc., Dexter MI
Scanner: Magitex 1875
Imagesetter: Purup Magnum
Press: (text) 40" Heidelberg Speedmaster ZP, (cover) 40" Heidelberg 501H-4C SM74
Printer: Thomson-Shore, Inc., Dexter MI
Cover Films: M&J Prepress, Albany NY
Map: Ron Toelke Associates, Chatham NY

For Els

Oh, East is East, and West is West, and never the twain shall meet,
Till Earth and Sky stand presently at God's great Judgment Seat;
But there is neither East nor West, Border, nor Breed, nor Birth,
When two strong men stand face to face, though they come
*   from the ends of the earth!*

Rudyard Kipling
Ballad of East and West, 1889

Contents

The sun and the air and the light are good in this place and have made me healthy as I never was in my life. . . . It's three miles from anywhere and wondrous self-contained. No one can get at you. . . .

Rudyard Kipling, in a September, 1892, letter from Vermont to British editor and essayist William Ernest Henley

Foreword

In 1892, when Rudyard Kipling first came to live in Vermont, he was himself much like the United States—brash, young, and swiftly becoming world famous.

As with many Englishmen of his day, Kipling looked down on the States, never imagining that in four years he would be back in England, thinking about America and wondering "how the deuce it has wound itself around my heartstrings the way it has."

During those productive years in Vermont, Kipling wrote *The Jungle Books*, his most enduring work, and on a remote hillside built a home named "Naulakha," a Hindustani term meaning "jewel beyond price." In this time, there was great joy for Rudyard, as two daughters were born to him and his American wife, Caroline. There was also great sorrow.

In the States, Kipling made some lifelong friends, but also bitter enemies, and when he left in 1896, never to return, it was under a cloud of insult and jealousy. By then, he was forever changed, more modest, somewhat wiser, and grateful: "Those four years in America will be blessed unto me for all my life," he wrote to an American friend.

Rudyard Kipling never came back to Vermont, but he often remembered that stony New England hillside, and he found himself longing "sometimes for a clear October morning with a touch of frost."

Stuart Murray
East Chatham, New York

Rudyard Kipling in 1899.

Prologue

In the winter of 1892, London lay chilled and rainy as an influenza epidemic raged through the city, killing so many people that there were not enough black horses available for funeral processions.

On January 18th, at the altar of All Souls' Church in fog-shrouded Langham Place, a young couple took their marriage vows before a congregation of only six: four men, a woman, and a boy. All Souls' was almost empty because most of the couple's friends and family were sick with influenza; and also because the groom had kept the wedding secret, especially secret from the press.

The groom was Joseph Rudyard Kipling, the new writer whose meteoric rise these past two years had made him an international celebrity, fair game for reporters. Though once a journalist himself, Kipling wanted no newspapermen swarming around All Souls' on his wedding day. He cherished privacy, and needed it now more than ever, for he and his bride, Caroline Balestier of Rochester, New York, were in mourning.

Bride and groom were heartbroken by the death a few weeks earlier of Wolcott Balestier, Caroline's older brother and Rudyard's best friend. Not yet thirty when he died of typhus on a trip to Germany, Wolcott had represented an American publisher, signing contracts with important British authors. Rudyard Kipling was his biggest catch of all.

Becoming close friends over the past year, Rudyard and Wolcott had collaborated on a novel called *The Naulahka, A Story of West and East,* about Americans adventuring in India. During this time, Rudyard fell in love with Carrie, as he called Caroline, but the courtship did not go smoothly, for she was completely devoted to advancing Wolcott's career. When Wolcott died, Carrie and Rudyard suddenly agreed to marry. Some thought this wedding was, more than anything else, an expression of their mutual love for Wolcott.

In the wedding party was the renowned American novelist, Henry James, who also had been a friend of Wolcott Balestier. As the closest male to Carrie's family in England, James gave away the bride, but he thought this was "a dreary little wedding" and had his doubts about the match.

After Wolcott's death, James had watched Carrie fight down sorrow as she grimly settled her brother's affairs. Startled by her controlled manner, James had written to a friend: ". . . poor little concentrated Carrie . . . is remarkable in her force, acuteness, capacity, and courage—and in the intense, almost manly nature of her emotion." In another letter, he wrote that Carrie was ". . . a hard, devoted, capable little person whom I don't in the least understand his marrying."

Despite the doubts of Henry James, Rudyard Kipling's future was full of promise. The author of widely acclaimed bestsellers, he was marrying the woman he loved, and they were to leave soon for a journey around the world. They would begin by crossing the United States, which Kipling knew well, having been there twice before. On the way, they would stop in Brattleboro, Vermont, where Carrie had family. Bride and groom were thinking seriously about returning to the States after their trip to make a home there.

Rudyard was willing enough to live in America, for he had been born in Bombay, India, of English parents, and had moved around so much during his life that his roots were not deep in any particular place. His first visit to the States had been in 1889, when he toured North America for almost six months. Although he liked much of what he saw, he considered America raw and lawless, immensely bountiful but arrogant and extravagant. He said so in widely published sarcastic essays that delighted British readers but caused resentment among Americans—especially American journalists, whom he publicly ridiculed.

Returning to England, Kipling continued to conflict with journalists. As his fame grew, they hounded him for copy, followed his every move, and time and again disturbed his privacy. By January, 1892, embittered against the entire profession, he avoided all reporters, even keeping his wedding secret.

At five foot six, Rudyard was short and stocky, broad of shoulder, and slightly stooped. With a strong cleft chin and already beginning to bald, he seemed more mature than his twenty-six years. His round, thick glasses were framed by black eyebrows and moustache, and his eyes, like Carrie's, were a piercing blue.

Three years older than her groom, Carrie was a small woman, with tiny hands and feet. Because she was still in mourning, she wore no wedding gown or bridal lace for the ceremony, just a simple brown dress that buttoned down the front. Her hair was brown, her plain features dominated by those intense blue eyes, bright in the dimness of the church.

Wolcott Balestier was Carrie's brother and Rudyard's best friend in England, collaborating with Kipling on the novel *The Naulahka* just before falling ill and dying on a trip to Germany.

When the brief ceremony was over, the Kiplings parted at the church door, Carrie to nurse her mother and sister—both lying ill with the flu in their London rooms—and Rudyard to write letters at his chambers across the street in Brown's Hotel. In one letter he told a cousin, "Never was anything less like a wedding," but he was "idiotically happy."

Later that day, Kipling was on his way to meet Carrie when he saw a large newspaper poster lying on the rainy sidewalk. He was dismayed to see its screaming headline announcing his marriage. He had failed, after all, to keep his wedding out of the papers.

Now he was even angrier at reporters, and frustrated to feel so utterly defenseless against them.

Caroline Balestier before marrying Rudyard in 1892.

It's north you may run to the rime-ringed sun
Or south to the blind Horn's hate;
Or east all the way into Mississippi Bay,
Or west to the Golden Gate;
Where the blindest bluffs hold good, dear heart,
And the wildest tales are true,
And the men bulk big on the old trail, our own trail, the out trail,
And Life runs large on the Long Trail—the trail that is always new.

The Long Trail, 1891

Chapter 1

Letters of Travel

Embarking from Liverpool on February 3, 1892, the newlywed Kiplings were happy and secure, with new books soon to be published, more than 2,000 pounds sterling in the bank, and berths on the North German ship S.S. *Teutonic* bound for New York. Thus began their "long trail," evoked in a poem Rudyard dedicated to Carrie.

They were seen off at the docks by their acquaintance, Bram Stoker, soon to write his horror novel, *Dracula*, and by Henry James. A keen admirer and patron of Kipling, James had supported his election to the Savile Club, the meeting place of literary society. He had written about Kipling to his friend, popular Scottish novelist Robert Louis Stevenson, who was living in the South Pacific, on Samoa.

James told Stevenson that Kipling was "the star of the hour" and Stevenson's "nascent rival." Stevenson replied, "Kipling is too clever to live." And: "Kipling is by far the most promising young man who has appeared since—ahem—I appeared."

As the Kiplings crossed the wintry, gale-tossed Atlantic, Rudyard expected the journey to take him eventually to Samoa and Stevenson, whose work he liked so much. This was the second time he had set out to meet Stevenson, the first being an aborted world voyage the previous summer, in 1891.

At that time, Kipling had broken down from overwork, suffering from chronically weak lungs that often ached in the damp English weather. He had taken a long sea journey for his health, departing England in August and heading south around Africa, then eastward to Asia. He had wanted Carrie to come along as his wife, but she had not been ready to marry.

He had traveled alone to South Africa, Australia, and on to New Zealand with hopes of taking a ship to Stevenson, who lived in the warm climate because of his own poor health. Difficulties with sailing schedules to Samoa had prevented that visit and Kipling had gone to India.

By December he was in Lahore, visiting his parents, Alice and Lockwood Kipling. It was a happy homecoming.

The elder Kiplings were "Anglo-Indians," as British nationals residing in the crown colony were called. Since 1865, the year Rudyard was born in Bombay, Lockwood had been an art instructor and museum curator employed by the colonial government.

As was common practice with Anglo-Indians, the Kiplings sent their son to England at the age of six for his elementary education. There, Rudyard lived unhappily with foster parents until he was twelve, then went to boarding school.

He returned to India at seventeen to work hard for seven years on provincial newspapers, rising to become a special correspondent with the freedom to rove the subcontinent, writing what he wished. From Bombay to the Himalayan foothills, Kipling followed frontier campaigns and engineering projects. He journeyed alone through dangerous unconquered country and endured the brutally hot climate that sometimes drove Europeans mad.

He once recklessly defied a local chieftain who tried to bribe him to write favorable articles that would make the chieftain look good to the British rulers. Kipling's refusal could have cost his life, but in the end the chieftain delighted in the young sahib's courage. Working long grueling hours as an editor in the sweltering newspaper plant, he more than once came down with fever that also brought him close to death.

In India, Kipling made his first mark as an author. Poems, essays, and short stories he wrote for the *Pioneer*, a newspaper based in the city of Allahabad, were collected and published as books back in Britain. He wrote insightfully about the most current and controversial topics of the day: the moral obligations of ruling the empire, the mistreatment of common soldiers by the upper classes, the true character of native peoples in the colonies, and the sometimes scandalous secret lives of Anglo-Indians and military men in India.

Kipling's fresh voice, revealing intimate details about a fascinating scene, won him a small but enthusiastic following, which included London's literary elite. He loved India, especially Bombay, but his restless ambition took him around the world to London. Upon his return to England late in 1889, he was sought out by publishers who wanted his work and by writers who wanted to know him.

Writing prolifically, Kipling burst upon the scene in early 1890. He became the rage in both the United States and the British Empire, his readers fascinated by his strong and irreverent writing, which crackled with anti-establishment humor.

Most famous for his short stories and galloping verses about the harsh life of lowly redcoats and devoted civil servants in the ranks of Her Majesty's colonial administration, Kipling often expressed himself in the crude, blunt voice of a private soldier—as no leading English author ever had before.

A recurring theme was the government's duty to the common man, British or colonial, white or native. Both intellectual society and music hall ruffians loved Kipling's poems and short stories. No one since Charles Dickens of three decades previous had so appealed to rich and poor alike.

Fired by lofty ideals, but cynical about the shortcomings of the often-blundering imperial administration he had seen firsthand, Kipling's opinions shook the foundations of the political establishment and infuriated even prime ministers. He composed inspirational, sometimes stinging, "public poetry" such as "The English Flag," which made the empire-building British look at themselves in a new and revealing mirror:

> *Winds of the World, give answer! They are whimpering to and fro—*
> *And what should they know of England who only England know?—*
> *The poor little street-bred people that vapour and fume and brag,*
> *They are lifting their heads in the stillness to yelp at the English Flag!*

Alfred Lord Tennyson, the aged British poet laureate (also known as a poet of the soldier and famous for his "The Charge of the Light Brigade") compared Kipling to the rest of the new generation of writers, saying he was "the only one of them with the divine fire." It was rumored that, on Tennyson's death, Kipling would be offered the title of poet laureate of the empire, an unprecedented honor, for he was much younger than any other leading man of letters.

Supremely confident in his powers as writer, social commentator, and poet, Kipling described in "Song of the Banjo" the spell he could weave:

> *And the tunes that mean so much to you alone—*
> *   Common tunes that make you choke and blow your nose,*
> *Vulgar tunes that bring the laugh that brings the groan—*
> *   I can rip your very heartstrings out with those;*
> *With the feasting and the folly and the fun—*
> *   And the lying and the lusting and the drink,*
> *And the merry play that drops you when you're done,*
> *   To the thoughts that burn like irons if you think.*

Filled with the same hunger for accomplishment that was urging the British Empire to reach its zenith in the next ten years, Kipling dreamed of the Anglo-Saxon race taming and civilizing the rest of the world—for what he considered to be the world's own good. The United States, he hoped, would be an ally of the British Empire. Until now, however, little of his work was calculated to win Americans to his point of view.

In 1889, when Kipling made that first globe-trotting journey from India to America, he paid his way by writing "letters of travel" essays for the *Pioneer*. In a glib and light-hearted style he told what he saw from Burma to China, Japan to California and the Wild West, from western Canada to Niagara Falls and the East Coast. The letters were also published by a Chicago newspaper, and soon were pirated by other papers and read everywhere in the United States.

Though Kipling liked Americans, he could not stand to hear them boast—as so many invariably and loudly did in those freewheeling days of expansion, speculation, gold rushes, and ready money. The first thing he did upon arriving in San Francisco was to write a letter of travel that made fun of the city's harbor defenses.

". . . I saw with great joy that the block-house which guarded the mouth of the 'finest harbor in the world, Sir,' could be silenced by two gunboats from Hong Kong with safety, comfort and despatch."

In another letter, Kipling quoted an anonymous American who supposedly told him that in the United States, "The whole system is rotten from top to bottom, as rotten as rotten can be." As for American politics, Kipling's American said, "No one but a low-down man will run for Congress. . . . If I had money enough I could buy the Senate of the United States, the Eagle and the Star-Spangled Banner complete." And: "With us our better classes are corrupt and our lower classes are lawless."

Another anonymous American warned Kipling not to carry a revolver unless he knew how to use it, or he might be drawn into deadly gunplay. Indeed, after some months touring the West, Kipling came to believe that in saloons he was safer keeping his hands always in sight than risk being shot by a drunk who might think he was going for a concealed revolver.

Of Chicago's lower depths, Kipling wrote, "Except in London . . . I had never seen such a collection of miserables." That he included the British capital in his critique did not count for much with annoyed American readers.

Kipling even twitted the American way of speaking: "They delude themselves into the belief that they talk English." He sneered at the small standing army: "When one hears so much of the nation that can whip the earth, it is . . . surprising to find her so temptingly spankable." As for the lack of forts on the lakeshore near Buffalo: ". . . an unarmoured gunboat guarding Toronto could ravage the towns on the lakes."

Kipling described a well-dressed American lady at Chicago's slaughterhouses, eagerly watching the butchery. He wrote that Salt Lake City's Mormons were lower-class practitioners of "tawdry mysticism" who borrowed from Freemasonry. And on reaching the East Coast, he guffawed in print that "three first-class ironclads would account for New York, Bartholdi's statue and all."

In fact, Kipling had cause for resentment of the United States, for American publishers had printed his books without his permission, and with no intention to remunerate him though his work sold even better there than in Britain. First published in England and India, his work was unprotected in the States because no international copyright law was yet in force.

Early in the 1889 visit, he admitted his remarks "may sound blood-thirsty, but remember, I had come with a grievance upon me—the grievance of pirated English books."

Though Kipling had plenty of good things to say about the States, such comments were either in personal letters or (because they were not controversial) were not reprinted by American papers. He especially admired American women: "I am hopelessly in love with about eight American maidens—all perfectly delightful till the next one comes into the room." He said, "They possess, moreover, a life among themselves, independent of any masculine associations . . . (and) they can take care of themselves."

Indeed, Kipling had for years been enchanted by an American woman who was living in India and was interested in his writing. She was, however, happily married. Later, he was informally and briefly engaged to a second American woman before marrying a third, Carrie Balestier.

Kipling was interested in all he could learn about Americans.

An excellent listener, he soaked up local color, dialects, mannerisms, and attitudes. His memory was uncanny, his powers of observation springing from a fascination with everything around him. Relentlessly striving for what he believed to be authenticity was a crucial aspect of his art.

Kipling took particular pride in honesty, cultivating an ability to look at things from opposite points of view, as he said in "The Two-sided Man":

Much I owe to the Lands that grew—
More to the Lives that fed—
But most to Allah Who gave me two
Separate sides to my head.

* * *

I would go without shirt or shoe,
Friend, tobacco or bread,
Sooner than lose for a minute the two
Separate sides of my head!

Despite his high standard of honesty—or perhaps because of it—the 1889 letters of travel too often made Kipling sound like a young know-it-all. His frank but shallow comments on the United States were resented as only an Englishman's comments could be resented by a nation which, more than a century after the Revolution, still had plenty of citizens who considered Britain an adversary.

During his visit, he spoke brashly to American reporters, naïvely providing controversial copy that sold newspapers. In a letter of travel he said the most persistent reporter "overwhelmed me not so much by his poignant audacity as by his beautiful ignorance." Talking to American reporters was "exactly like talking to a child—a very rude little child." No matter how an answer was given, he said, the reporter simply could not understand it.

When one in San Francisco asked, "Have you got reporters anything like our reporters on Indian newspapers?" Kipling said no. "They would die."

American newspaper editors gleefully quoted his most outrageous letters of travel. Sometimes, false passages were inserted to make Kipling all the more arrogant and despicable in American eyes. With much fanfare these editors played on anti-British sentiment for all it was worth and published editorials and letters that attacked Kipling ferociously. Angered, he eventually refused to be interviewed, further irritating American journalists.

In the spring of 1891, Kipling made his second visit to the States, a brief holiday in New York City to visit an uncle who lived there. The moment he landed, he again was sought by reporters who wanted interviews more than ever now that he was famous. He refused, infuriating reporters and editors, who swore to get even if he ever came back.

The years 1890–91 in England were a whirlwind of work and triumph, which left Kipling ill and exhausted, on the verge of a nervous collapse by the time he went on that sea voyage in 1891.

At the end of December, while with his mother and father in India, he received a telegram from Carrie with the devastating news that Wolcott had died in Germany. Kipling cut short his world trip, rushing back to London, and on the way telegraphed a proposal of marriage to Carrie. He reached England on January 10, 1892, and eight days later, with a special license permitting a shorter waiting period, they took their vows in All Souls'.

Now, in early February, Kipling's next journey around the world did include Carrie, and this time they surely would get to Samoa and Robert Louis Stevenson, who also had an American wife.

Both to the road again, again!
Out on a clean sea-track—
Follow the cross of the gipsy trail
Over the world and back!

* * *

"The wild hawk to the windswept sky,
The deer to the wholesome wold
And the heart of a man to the heart of a maid,
As it was in the days of old."

The heart of a man to the heart of a maid—
Light of my tents be fleet.
Morning waits at the end of the world,
And the world is all at our feet!

The Gipsy Trail, 1892

Chapter 2

In Sight of Monadnock

The weather was dark and cold on the 1892 Atlantic crossing to New York, but Rudyard's irrepressible personality cheered up fellow passengers on the liner.

Known as Ruddy or Rud to friends and family, Kipling loved good company and witty conversation. At table on the ship he always was ready with a store of colorful tales from India, and while puffing on his briar pipe could hold forth for hours in receptive company. A brilliant raconteur, quick at composing verse on the spot, his personal magnetism and wit made him new American friends whom he would know for the rest of his life.

On the S.S. *Teutonic* he was a favorite companion of writer and diplomat John Hay, the former secretary to Abraham Lincoln, and of essayist Henry Adams, who wrote, "Fate was kind on that voyage. Rudyard Kipling . . . dashed over the passenger his exuberant fountain of gaiety and wit—as though playing a garden hose on a thirsty and faded begonia."

With unmatched literary success behind him and prospects of even greater success to come, Kipling entered married life, feeling himself to be master of all he saw.

On February 11, 1892, the ship steamed out of the gloomy Atlantic and into New York harbor, which was basking in glorious winter sunlight.

At the Manhattan docks, reporters swarmed around the customs station, unsuccessfully looking for Kipling, who avoided them. They later came hat-in-hand to his hotel, but again he refused to be interviewed. Carrie was his first line of defense, and a formidable one. Used to working tirelessly for Wolcott, she now turned her efforts to supporting and protecting Rudyard's writing career.

From the start, Carrie brought order into her husband's busy and somewhat disheveled life, shielding him from intrusions into his favorite writing time, 9 a.m. to 1 p.m. Thanks to her, Kipling had been able to write the last few pages of his and Wolcott's novel, *The Naulahka*, even while surrounded by the spirited S.S. *Teutonic* passengers.

Henry Wolcott Balestier, Carrie's father, was from Chicago and had well-to-do French Huguenot and New England forebears.

Anna Smith Balestier, Carrie's mother, was the daughter of an internationally eminent attorney, who settled in Rochester, N.Y.

Caroline Balestier Kipling came from a world far different from that of her husband, who had two Methodist ministers as grandfathers and a mingling of Scottish and English blood. Not only was Carrie American born, but on the Balestier side of her lineage were French Huguenots who fled religious persecution in France. One generation had lived in the West Indies before emigrating to the United States, where the family prospered.

Born in Rochester on December 31, 1862—Rudyard's birthday was December 30th—Carrie was the second of four children. Her widowed mother, the former Anna Smith, was from a leading New England family that could count among its luminaries three Connecticut governors, a daughter of Paul Revere, a signatory to the Declaration of Independence, and most recently a legal advisor to the Japanese Mikado.

Wealthy, observing strict manners that set the family apart from less formal neighbors, the Balestiers always dressed for dinner and were known for favoring imported wines. Of all the Balestier children, Carrie in particular liked to observe genteel formality, but in contrast with this reserved side of her nature was a strong and spontaneous creative impulse.

From girlhood, Carrie had a tendency to daydream, to become so lost in thought that she gave the appearance of living in a world of her own. In her teens she and Wolcott, whom she adored, made sure to sport the most outrageously gaudy clothing as an expression of their individualism. Carrie painted watercolors and wrote poetry; her poem "The Chimes of Cornell" was published in the *Cornell Review* when Wolcott was a student there.

Love of art and writing united Carrie with Wolcott, and later with Rudyard. She had done all she could to promote Wolcott's career in publishing. His ability to earn the loyalty of writers won him repute soon after he arrived in England in 1888, and he was regarded by Henry James as a keen young man with a bright future. In 1889, Carrie came to London with her mother, Anna, younger sister, Josephine, and her fun-loving younger brother, Beatty, with his beautiful new wife, Mai. At first, there were hopes of bringing Beatty into the publishing business, but to Wolcott's and Carrie's sore disappointment, he proved to be a genial drunkard.

Though dynamic and clever, he had a reputation for staggering, tipsy, through London's alehouses, dressed in a fur coat, wearing a hat with a great feather fluttering from it, and dragged by a set of leashed wolfhounds. It did not matter that he was so well liked by English friends, for Beatty became an embarrassment to his cultivated brother and sister. Carrie soon turned cold to Mai, who was no help in curbing Beatty's wildness. Very much at the wish of Carrie, he and Mai were quietly sent home. Yet Beatty was dear to his family, and Wolcott worried to the end about his welfare.

Now, as Rudyard and Carrie began their wedding journey, over them hung Wolcott's final wish that they look after Beatty, then living with Mai and an infant daughter at the Balestier estate near Brattleboro, Vermont. According to what the Kiplings had heard from Carrie's family, he was still drinking heavily.

Resolved to do their best for him, the Kiplings would visit Beatty before continuing their globe-trotting, but what could be done, they did not yet know.

After bleak England and the cloudy ocean voyage, Rudyard appreciated the clear, dry weather that met him in New York City, describing it as a "flood of winter sunshine that made unaccustomed eyelids blink."

The Kiplings stayed at the Brunswick Hotel on Madison Square, around which Rudyard and Carrie enjoyed walking, observing the "beautifully dressed babies playing counting-out games." The newlyweds "were content, and more than content to drift aimlessly up and down the brilliant streets, wondering a little why the finest light should be wasted on the worst pavements in the world."

Once again Rudyard wrote letters of travel, now for the *Times* of London and for simultaneous publication in the *New York Sun*. As in his 1889 letters, his opinions of America were often biting, but he was seasoned with more wisdom and patience and did not rant as he had three years earlier. His harshest comments were for the New York City streets:

"Gullies, holes, ruts, cobble-stones awry, kerbstones rising from two to six inches above the level of slatternly pavements; tram-lines from two to three inches above street levels; building materials scattered half across the street; lime boards, cut stone, and ash barrels generally and generously everywhere; wheeled traffic taking its chances, dray versus brougham, at crossroads. . . ."

Rudyard and Carrie planned to spend some weeks in New York, arranging matters with book and magazine editors who wanted to publish his works. First, however, five days after their arrival, they took a train two hundred miles north to Brattleboro. The Balestier family made its home in Rochester, New York, but Carrie's and Wolcott's generation had a soft spot for Brattleboro, a country town where they had spent summers as children visiting their wealthy widowed grandmother, "Madam" Caroline Balestier. Since 1868, Brattleboro, with its 6,000 inhabitants, had been the summer home of the family matriarch, whose farm was three miles north of town. With Beatty and Mai now also living there, Brattleboro was considered the center of Balestier family life.

Until the middle of the century, Brattleboro had been a thriving resort and health spa where folk came for the "water cure" that was especially popular with the Eastern and Southern elite. The Civil War shattered the class and social structure of the United States, reducing the Southern clientele who once had been so prominent among those coming for the cure. The loss of Southerners was a blow to the spa, a problem made worse when it became more fashionable to sail to Europe for a holiday than to visit American resorts. By 1892, Brattleboro had lost its luster, but still attracted a fair number of well-to-do outsiders who vacationed there or built seasonal homes nearby.

Of his trip by rail to Brattleboro, Kipling wrote: "So New York passed away upon a sunny afternoon, with her roar and rattle, her complex smells, her triply overheated rooms, and much too energetic inhabitants, while the train went north to the lands where the snow lay."

Such snow and bitter cold astonished the India-born Rudyard Kipling as, just after midnight on February 17th, the train drew into sleeping Brattleboro.

"Thirty below freezing! It was inconceivable till one stepped out into it at midnight, and the first shock of that clear, still air took away the breath as does a plunge into seawater."

Beatty Balestier was there to take them home from the station. Full as ever of good cheer and rough humor, Beatty was bundled in furs on the driver's perch of a horse-drawn sleigh, looking to Kipling like "a walrus sitting on a woolpack."

From the start, Kipling enjoyed the open hospitality of his loud-talking brother-in-law, who "wrapped us in hairy goatskin coats, caps that came down over the ears, buffalo robes and blankets, and yet more buffalo robes till we, too, looked like walruses and moved almost as gracefully."

Off they went through the hushed town, skimming out of Main Street to the jingle of sleigh bells. In bright moonlight, the countryside lay under a blanket of snow as they passed along the western bank of the ice-bound Connecticut River. If not for the sleigh bells, said Kipling, the "ride might have taken place in a dream, for there was no sound of hoofs upon the snow, the runners sighed a little now and again as they glided over an inequality, and all the sheeted hills round about were dumb as death."

This moonlit ride past snowdrifts up "to the level of the stone fences or curling over their tops in a lip of frosted silver" was "beautiful beyond expression." It was more than the loveliness of the night that thrilled Kipling, however: he knew that somewhere in the eastern distance rose Mount Monadnock, the subject of a famous poem by Ralph Waldo Emerson.

During schoolboy days, Kipling had read that poem, which left him with the idea of the mountain being a "wise old giant . . . who makes us sane and sober and free from little things if we trust him."

In "Monadnoc," Emerson wrote:

> Man in these crags a fastness find
> To fight pollution of the mind.
>   * * *
> Hither we bring Our insect miseries to thy rocks;
> And the whole flight, with folded wing,
> Vanish, and end their murmuring,—
> Vanish beside these dedicated blocks,
> Which who can tell what mason laid?

The Kiplings spent the night at Beatty's farmhouse on an isolated road in Dummerston, north of Brattleboro. The next morning Rudyard was eager to hike up a hillside and look on while Monadnock "heeds his sky affairs," as Emerson described it. Rudyard and Carrie set out with Beatty to find a view of the mountain, and in cold sunlight walked up the plowed road from Beatty's farm, called Maple-wood, a property given to him by his grandmother, Madam Balestier.

After the hauntingly lovely night, Kipling was inspired by the contrasting beauty of a Vermont winter's day. He would write in his next letter of travel that "the other side of the picture was revealed in the colours of the sunlight. There was never a cloud in the sky that rested on the snow-line of the horizon as a sapphire on white velvet."

They stopped at the tree-lined edge of a meadow sloping down to the east, and saw, thirty miles away in New Hampshire, the tip of Monadnock. The essay recalls the sight: "Beyond the very furthest range, where the pines turn to a faint blue haze against the one solitary peak—a real mountain, and not a hill—showed like a gigantic thumbnail pointing heavenward."

Looking at the blue-gray top of distant Monadnock was a special moment for Kipling, pleased to be in this natural setting so lovely and tranquil, a setting Emerson himself might have had in mind when he wrote "Monadnoc":

> *"Happy," I said, "whose home is here!*
> *Fair fortunes to the mountaineer!*
> *Boon Nature to his poorest shed*
> *Has royal pleasure-grounds outspread."*

In the essay, Kipling recalled that as a youth, "Monadnock came to mean everything that was helpful, healing, and full of quiet, and when I saw him half across New Hampshire, he did not fail. In utter stillness a hemlock bough, over-weighted with snow, came down a foot or two with a tired little sigh; the snow slid off and the little branch flew nodding back to its fellows."

As a boy, he had first heard the word Monadnock in *The Echo Club*, a book by Bayard Taylor containing what Kipling called "a shameless parody of Emerson's style, before ever style or verse had interest for me. But the word stuck because of a rhyme, in which one was

> *. . . crowned coeval*
> *With Monandoc's crest,*
> *And my wings extended*
> *Touch the East and West."*

In this high place, touching East and West, the Man of the East was profound-ly moved to be standing "In Sight of Monadnock," the title of his letter of travel. As the Kiplings and Beatty admired the view, another fellow appeared on the hillside, flapping across the drifts on snowshoes. This was Will Cabot, a young man who had been close friends with Wolcott Balestier. In fact, Cabot's sister Mary, called "Molly," had been in love with Wolcott. Cabot knew about the Kipling-Balestier collaboration on the novel *The Naulahka*, which for months had been appearing serially in *Century Magazine*.

Almost all Brattleboro had read an article in the *Vermont Phoenix*, the local weekly, about Kipling's friendship with Wolcott. Published last November, shortly before Wolcott died, the article had been written by Will Cabot, who had firsthand information about the community's favorite son in London. Not only was his sister Molly corresponding with Wolcott, but another Brattleboro man was one of Wolcott's assistants and could be counted on for news from time to time.

Not all Cabot's facts were right, however, and it must have been a surprise for Kipling to learn that the locals believed he had been a struggling failure "with a great pile of unpublished manuscripts" in his India trunk when he first met Wolcott in London. It was thought hereabouts that Wolcott had made Kipling a success, and that immediately after *The Naulahka* began to appear in *Century*, Rudyard "awoke one morning to find himself famous."

No one here seemed to know that Kipling had been famous before he met Wolcott. Such misconceptions, however, were understandable in the hometown of a celebrity, and Kipling was content that his dear friend was remembered in Brattleboro with such admiration. He let it all pass without remark and proceeded to sport about in the snow, trying on Cabot's snowshoes.

"The gigantic lawn-tennis bats strung with hide are not easy to maneuver," he wrote. "When you . . . can slide one shoe above the other deftly . . . the sensation of paddling over a ten-foot-deep drift and taking short-cuts by buried fences is worth the ankle-ache."

Later, "For the honor of Monadnock there was made . . . an image of snow of Guatama Buddah, something too squat and not altogether equal on both sides, but with an imperial and reposeful waist."

On that enjoyable day, Rudyard and Carrie decided they would, indeed, make a home here when they returned from their world tour. What better spot to build upon than this hillside facing Mount Monadnock? Here, Kipling could work in pure isolation, if he wished, far from the hustle and noise of London's literary world. And for his weak lungs, Vermont's climate was much more healthful.

The land the Kiplings wanted for their house belonged to Beatty, who with his usual generosity immediately offered to share it with them, no purchase being necessary.

The Law whereby my Lady moves
Was never Law to me,
But 'tis enough that she approves
Whatever Law it be.

For in the Law and by that Law
My constant course I'll steer;
Not that I heed or deem it dread,
But that she holds it dear.

Tho' Asia sent for my content
Her richest argosies,
Those would I spurn and bid return
If that should give her ease.

My Lady's Law, 1892
Chapter heading for *The Naulahka*

Chapter 3

The Last Time East of Suez

Beatty Balestier was by calculated choice very different from his smoothly sophisticated brother, Wolcott. If Kipling was a Man of the East, then garrulous, cider-slugging Beatty was a Man of the West. Rudyard's years as a journalist in India, familiar with the British troops, gave him some understanding of men as bluff and hearty as Beatty, and he enjoyed their company.

Beatty was short, about Kipling's size, but very strong and vigorous, with a jaunty gait. Though he carried no revolver in the way of the Wild West characters Kipling had met on his earlier tour of America, he was an avid outdoorsman and hunter, and expert with horses. He always wore a hat cocked over his right ear, and was usually jovial, blasphemous, and humorous.

Incomparable as a worker when he wanted to be, he was indolent and procrastinating when it suited him—which it did too often for his own good. He had Maplewood because of the doting affection of his grandmother, Madam Balestier, whose home, a little down the road, was a handsome colonial mansion known as Beechwood. She had given Beatty the farm because he was her favorite and most charming grandchild.

A well-read intellectual after his own fashion, Beatty was, like Kipling, a marvelous raconteur. He had an uncanny ability to meet a person on his or her own level, cultured or uncultured or in between. Yet his anger could be as sudden as his kindness was generous. It was said he had a "tongue like a skinning knife" when in a fury. Among his particular dislikes were penny-pinching, snobbishness, and social climbing—characteristics he attributed to his more conservative sister, Carrie. Furthermore, unlike him, she always carefully managed her financial resources.

Beatty's extravagance and downright laziness combined with periodic drinking binges to make people's heads wag, but they readily excused him. "That's Beatty," they would say, and welcomed him into their homes.

Beatty liked to drink in cheerful company, and willingly shared his last drop. Everyone was welcome at his table, passersby on the road or crossing a meadow

Beatty Balestier at Beechwood, his farm near the Kiplings at Naulakha.

often being hailed with a clanging of Beatty's porch bell and a shout to "Come and have a drink, goddammit!" A typical example of his generosity—which went hand-in-hand with the bad business management that often kept him broke—was when he once grew peaches that were "too beautiful to sell," so he gave them away. Beatty invariably drove his buckboard and team at a breakneck gallop along country roads, over covered bridges, and into Brattleboro's streets. Sometimes, when drunk, he raced through town like a chariot driver, and one Sunday, when trying to bring a friend to the train station on time, he turned his wagon over on Main Street.

In winter, Beatty drove so fast along roads hemmed in with steep banks of plowed snow, that children in Dummerston and Brattleboro were warned to leap out of the way whenever they heard his recognizably loud sleigh bells approaching. He entered sleigh races across the frozen Connecticut River, from the Vermont side to the tavern at Chesterfield, New Hampshire. On one occasion the prize was a case of champagne—to be polished off on the spot.

Frederic F. Van de Water, a friend of later years, wrote of Beatty: "He could never refrain from the grand gesture. . . . He could not grip a whip without cracking it or raise a glass without draining it. . . .

"He was a black sheep who wore that title proudly. He was a pain to the pious, a thorn to the respectable, an affront to the abstemious. He had a brilliant mind that he refused to harness for profitable toil; a will that mocked all scruple or stricture. He was iconoclast, spendthrift, roysterer, bitter enemy, charming and generous friend. He loved horses and liquor, strife and revelry. Beatty trampled and shouldered his own path through life and when the bills for trespass came due, he suffered their mounting pressure without protest or self-pity."

The Beatty Balestier of February, 1892, seemed on the way to earning the reputation of a ne'er-do-well, and the Kiplings dreaded that. When Beatty cheerfully offered to share ownership of the land with them, Carrie suggested instead the Kiplings take over his farm and finance him, for he always needed cash. In this way, she thought, they could look after him and his family and at the same time help manage the business side of his farm.

Too proud to accept those terms, and somewhat annoyed at such a patronizing proposal, the independent-minded Beatty flatly declined to turn over the farm. When the Kiplings then asked to buy eleven acres outright, with a proper contract of sale and subdivision, he agreed, as long as he kept a right of way across the meadow and the haying rights. Good fields were scarce in this stony country of steep slopes and maple forest. (Beatty was paid $750, but no written contract exists granting him haying rights or right of way.)

The Kiplings then proposed that Beatty manage the construction of their home on the site, which was just across the line in the town of Dummerston. He could be sure of a good income from the project for many months to come, and would earn his pay rather than feel he was being kept by his wealthy sister and her famous English husband.

It was all soon agreed upon, and Beatty was to join Rudyard and Carrie in New York City to arrange the legal paperwork. Also in New York was Henry Rutgers Marshall, an architect friend of the Balestiers, who would begin the design of their new home. The excavation and fieldstone foundation of the house would be started before the onset of next winter, and when the Kiplings returned from their journey in spring of 1893, they would be on hand for the actual construction.

Completing this arrangement was a happy occasion, as much for the Kiplings as for Beatty, who liked the idea of his sister living so close. On this visit, his wife Mai and Carrie got along in spite of the friction they had experienced in England, when Carrie had insisted Beatty and Mai return home. Rudyard was particularly taken by Beatty's year-old daughter, Marjorie, for he loved children, often telling them stories and playing with them for hours.

At last, the Kiplings could genuinely hope Beatty would have the stability to mend his ways. When they returned to Vermont, he would be subject to Carrie's oversight, and she fully intended, in accordance with Wolcott's last wish, to help Beatty make something of himself, once and for all.

On February 20, 1892, Rudyard and Carrie Kipling returned by train southward to New York, where they stayed a few more weeks, residing in a boarding house at 11 East 32nd Street. He had editors to visit and poems and essays to write, including the letter of travel, "In Sight of Monadnock."

During his brief visit to southern Vermont, Rudyard had met a few residents, spending time observing and absorbing local color, as he loved to do wherever he was. He appreciated the natural beauty around Brattleboro, but some of what he saw of the people did not appeal to him, as he told his readers:

"There is so much, so very much to write, if it were worth while, about that queer little town by the railway station, with its life running, to all outward seeming, as smoothly as the hack-coupes on their sleigh mounting, and within disturbed by the hatreds and troubles and jealousies that vex the minds of all but the gods."

This condition, Kipling said, was much the same in small towns the world over—and he had seen many in his travels from India to Australia, the Far East, America, Africa, Europe, and back again. He was especially uncomfortable with the American tendency to pry into another's private affairs, even those of a stranger.

He said of Brattleboro, "You realise the atmosphere when you read in the local paper announcements of 'chicken suppers' and 'church sociables' to be given by such and such a denomination, sandwiched between paragraphs of genial and friendly interest, showing that the countryside live (and without slaying each other) on terms of terrifying intimacy."

Such intimacy was distasteful to Kipling, although ironically his own letters of travel were much the same sort of idle gossip, the impressions of an opinionated globe-trotter. Years before in India he had been repelled by globe-trotters, sneering at "the man who 'does' kingdoms in days and writes books upon them in weeks."

Now in 1892, as in his 1889 globe-trotting travels, he had no qualms about passing snap judgments on Brattleboro, though he had spent just three days there.

In that next letter of travel he said he could relate much local gossip, but would not because "it is better to remember the lesson (of) Monadnock, and Emerson has said, 'Zeus hates busybodies. . . .'" He then proceeded to gossip as he described two farmers calling to each other "in a long, nasal drawl" from opposite sides of the street, one loudly giving his opinion about a neighbor and then concluding for all to hear: "But them there Andersons, they ain't got no notion of etikwette."

Kipling went on to say outsiders from "Boston and the like" perplexed the locals by building country homes on remote roads, far from the convenience of "Main Street," the term he coined for any small town. Although native Vermonters had little to do with outsiders, the natives seemed to know all about them: "Their dresses, their cattle, their views, the manners of their children, their manner towards their servants, and every other conceivable thing, is reported, digested, discussed, and rediscussed up and down Main Street."

Soon, Rudyard Kipling would be one of those outsiders building a house on a back road, far from the terrifying intimacy of Main Street.

Through March, 1892, Kipling attended to literary business from his rooming house in New York, including going over page proofs for the novel *The Naulahka*.

The title was a misspelling. It should have been "naulakha," a Hindi word meaning "nine lakher," a lakh being 100,000 rupees, and "naulakha" being a term for something of great value. In the novel, the American hero wants to acquire a fabulous Indian jewel, "The Naulahka." Kipling, himself, had made the first spelling mistake in a letter to Wolcott confirming their shared ownership of the book's rights. The misspelled version was published as the title, and for some unknown reason was never corrected by Kipling.

So the book had been written with one Balestier brother, and the house would be built with the other brother and a sister. Carrie suggested it be called "Crow's Nest" or perhaps "Liberty Hall." Rudyard, however, wanted to name it, too, "The Naulakha"—but with the proper spelling.

By the time the book, *The Naulahka*, was finished, Kipling was thinking about another story set in India, this one for children. He was creating a new character—a boy named Mowgli, who had been adopted by wolves and raised in the jungle among wild creatures wise and wicked, foolish and cruel. The jungle boy, Mowgli, had already appeared in an earlier Kipling story about India, "In the Rukh." The character of Mowgli first had occurred to Kipling as a result of a scene in *Nada the Lily*, H. Rider Haggard's African adventure story of a few years earlier, in which a character runs with a pack of wolves.

Kipling also was inspired by a book his father had recently published, entitled *Beast and Man in India*. John Lockwood Kipling, above all others, was his son's most respected and sternest critic, the one who judged whether a tale worked, particularly a tale set in India. Lockwood was a rich source of lore about the peoples and nature of India, which he had studied throughout his almost thirty years there. A fine writer, he was also an excellent artist, his specialty sculpture—especially bas relief illustrations.

Beast and Man in India is an abundant miscellany of information and observation, including folklore, myth, anthropology, and descriptions of flora and fauna, all colorfully interspersed with anecdotes and legends and decorated with Lockwood Kipling's art. Lockwood included many of his son's verses in the book, and Rudyard, in turn, was stimulated by the settings and potential characters his father described.

Charles Carrington, Kipling's biographer, said the book held the trove from which Rudyard developed *The Jungle Books*: "Here you may find Chil the kite and Tabaqui the jackal, the method of catching crows by a decoy, the nursery song about the wild plums in the jungle, the behaviour of snake and mongoose around the house, the . . . legends of the place where the elephants dance . . . the customs of the *bandar-log*."

Thus, in a broad panorama interpreted and selected by his father and also illustrated by Lockwood in pen-and-ink, Rudyard Kipling had the subjects of stories he would tell as *The Jungle Books*, his most enduring creation. These stories were born from the spirit of his father's book; they cast a respectful glance at Aesop's Fables, and owed much to the Jakata Tales, ancient Hindu parables that have been compared with Aesop.

Kipling was not yet ready to write about Mowgli, but verses were singing in his head that spring and images awaited the irresistible urge of his "daemon," as he termed the intuitive power that inspired his best work.

On March 26th Rudyard and Carrie set out from New York, traveling by train across North America on the next phase of their wedding journey. He planned to write the Mowgli stories when they returned to a permanent home in Vermont.

In a letter dated that day to an editor at *Century Magazine*, he said, ". . . we will be back again and have good times not as birds of passage but settled down citizens of the United States."

They covered much the same ground he had crossed in 1889. He had fond memories of that bachelor's footloose visit, when he had found his way to Elmira, New York, to pay an unannounced visit to Samuel Clemens, who as Mark Twain was one of his many American literary idols. From school days, Kipling had loved the work of American writers: Twain, Emerson, Bret Harte, Walt Whitman, and Joel Chandler Harris (author of the Uncle Remus stories).

Twain later wrote about that 1889 encounter with a talkative young Englishman not yet known to him: "I believed that he knew more than any person I had met before, and I knew that he knew that I knew less than any person he had met before—though he did not say it, and I was not expecting that he would."

Twain said to his wife: "Between us we cover all knowledge; he knows all that can be known, and I know the rest."

A Kipling letter of travel back then recorded that visit with a glow of awe and admiration: ". . . I have seen Mark Twain this golden morning, have shaken his hand and smoked a cigar—no two cigars—with him, and talked with him for more than two hours! . . . I was smoking his cigar, and I was hearing him talk— this man I had learned to love and admire fourteen thousand miles away."

Twain's daughter, Susy Clemens, was fascinated by Kipling, and kept his card as a memento. A year later, a friend of the family brought them a best-selling book of collected stories entitled *Plain Tales from the Hills*, by a new author, Rudyard Kipling. Susy ran to her room for the card. With surprise she realized the author—who, as Twain said "became suddenly known and universally known"— was the same young Englishman who had appeared in Elmira.

By 1892, Rudyard Kipling was as famous around the world as Mark Twain. Kipling's books were translated so often and in so many languages that he could not keep track of them. All the way across America, newspapermen heard of his and Carrie's coming and appeared at stations and hotels to ask for interviews. They all were summarily turned down by Carrie, now squarely at the fore as her husband's business manager.

The Kiplings passed through Chicago, Minneapolis, Winnipeg, and Vancouver, where they were to take ship for Japan. In Vancouver, they received the bad news that his purchase of land there in 1889 had been fraudulent, and he owned nothing, even though he had paid taxes on it these three years. Kipling laughed off this minor loss and they sailed across the Pacific, reaching Japan on April 20th.

Since Carrie was the granddaughter of a former American legal advisor to the Mikado, they were received with honor wherever they went in Japan. After a delightful stay, and as they contemplated going on to Samoa and Stevenson, they experienced two earthquakes: a mild natural one that caused them to flee excitedly into their hotel's garden and wait until it was over; and a disastrous financial one.

On the afternoon of June 9th, Kipling went to the Yokohama branch of his bank, the Oriental Banking Company, to draw out cash and was told it had just failed. All their savings—more than 2,000 pounds sterling—was lost. The only cash left was yen to the value of ten pounds sterling. As for the rest, they had reservations for Samoa, tickets back to Vancouver, and $100 in a New York bank. Furthermore, Carrie was expecting a baby.

"I returned with the news to my bride of three months and a child to be born," Kipling wrote in his autobiography. "There was an instant Committee of Ways and Means, which advanced our understanding of each other more than a cycle of solvent matrimony."

Rudyard and Carrie were drawn close by the ordeal. As they pondered their next step, waiting in their hotel room for the bank to clarify matters of future settlement, they endlessly played card games, mostly casino, which Carrie usually won. At last, the choice was made to turn back and head for Vermont.

"Retreat—flight if you like—was indicated." They cancelled their Thomas Cook Company travel reservations for Samoa and Robert Louis Stevenson. "What would Cook return for the tickets, not including the price of lost dreams?" To their relief, the fares to Samoa were generously refunded in full by Cook. Again, plans to visit Stevenson were aborted because of a crisis.

This was Rudyard's final visit to Asia, his birthplace and once his home. India, its lore and mysticism, would always remain in his heart, and its memories would pour into his work of the next few years, most of it written in America. As his biographer, Carrington, put it: "Never again did he take ship east of Suez."

No longer a wealthy couple on an exhilarating and carefree wedding tour, the Kiplings were broke, and faced grim immediate decisions about a future that had seemed so secure.

Kipling's illustration for "The Elephant's Child"

They could not see. Our flanking walls were wide,
     Hidden in a forest: where the bamboos bend
The great teak lumbers hemmed them either side.
          We drove them to the end,
Ay, to the Keddah where the last gate falls,
     The spears are brandished and the ropes are cast,
The torches flare between the brushwood walls
          And all the herd is fast: The Elephants of the Dom.

The great hearts trumpet and the paths are strait . . .

In the Keddah
Unfinished, 1892

Chapter 4

Time, Light, and Quiet

In Rudyard's honor, the Canadian railways carried them overland as complimentary guests. On this journey, he wrote an essay about the Northwest—the seal hunters, the gutsy developers of boom towns, and the ambitious explorers. He entitled it "Captains Courageous" in homage to them and wrote, "It is the next century that, in looking over its own, will see the heroes of our time clearly."

At midsummer the Kiplings reached Montreal, where Rudyard riled the city's luminaries, who were rebuffed when they invited him to a reception at the Pen and Pencil Club, "one of the most exclusive in the city," according to a local paper, which declared: "Montreal has had a snubbing such as it is little used to from the eccentric and conceited Indian novelist, Rudyard Kipling. . . . Although a number of prominent citizens wished to make the novelist's visit pleasant and called on him, Kipling haughtily refused to receive even their cards, and would see no one."

Kipling was called "ungentlemanly." The Montrealers could not have known either Kipling's personal distress or his profound affection for Canada, which he admired as the "elder daughter" of the empire.

A telegram from Caroline's grandmother, Madam Balestier, reached them in Montreal, saying they could rent a cottage on her road for ten dollars a month, about two pounds sterling. It would do while the new house was being built nearby, so they agreed to take it.

The place was known as Bliss Cottage, normally used by a hired man, and it stood on the farm owned by a family of that name. Kipling was not the first writer to work at Bliss Cottage. A few years before, the playwright Steele MacKaye, boarding nearby for the summer, had used the cottage as a studio for privacy. There he had written his well-known and critically successful *Paul Kauvan*, a play about the French Revolution.

The Kiplings got to Brattleboro on July 26th, at first staying with Beatty until the rented house became available in August. Years later Kipling wrote of southern Vermont as he found it then: "The country was large-boned, mountainous, wooded, and divided into farms of from fifty to two hundred barren acres. Roads, sketched in dirt, connected white, clap-boarded farmhouses. . . .

Bliss Cottage, in the Town of Brattleboro, was rented by the Kiplings for their first winter in Vermont, 1893–94.

There were many abandoned houses too; some decaying where they stood; others already reduced to a stone chimney-stack or mere green dimples still held by an un-defeated lilac bush."

He loved it. Carrie, too, was happy to be here again. She had come back to Vermont in time to see the late-summer meadows and roadsides bright with gold-enrod, a favorite of hers. Goldenrod was native to this country, but did not grow wild in England.

Soon after they arrived back in Vermont, Kipling found that hostility from newspapers had followed him to New England. The *Republican* of Springfield, Massachusetts, announced he had moved in: "It must really be hoped that Mr. Kipling will become acquainted with the B'boro people. It would broaden and deepen his mind and greatly improve his manners."

Despite the occasional surliness of American newspapers toward him, Kipling was pleased to be in Vermont, especially because work was starting on the road and site for Naulakha. He and Carrie went down to New York to meet with architect H.R. Marshall, who would come up in September to discuss the final plans. Kipling wanted the house built high on the meadow, in sight of the distant blue tip of Emerson's Mount Monadnock.

Their finances were not as bad as they might have been. Kipling's failed bank worked out a plan for settling its accounts by offering shares. Further, royalties were expected from the sales of *The Naulahka*, and from collections of short stories, including the immensely popular *Barrack-room Ballads*. There also was income from essays such as those in *Letters of Marque*, about his world travels.

Kipling happily resumed "the worship of Marjorie," Beatty's infant daughter. Contentment in the company of little Marjorie was stronger than ever now that Carrie was pregnant with their own first child.

"We've been fighting with a raw and empty cottage for the past four days, and have at last managed to lick it into something like shape," Rudyard wrote in August to Meta and Lockwood de Forest, family friends from his days in India, who now lived on Long Island.

Rudyard and Carrie labored to clean, paint, and furnish "with simplicity" their new home in time for winter and for the coming baby. They hired a Swedish maid, Anna Anderson, recently arrived in the States, and Carrie went about "hunting servants." With or without servants, Carrie was herself a hard worker, full of energy, and "imperially organizing the house," as Rudyard told publisher William Heinemann in a letter to England.

"I'm settling down in a house and my soul is divided between painting floors and hunting for lost gimlets. It is an employment that leaves very little time for the fine arts or literature."

He added, "I've a host of things to do and I must have time to write 'em in—time, light and quiet—three things that are hard to come by in London."

After ten years of steady, almost obsessive, writing of newspaper articles, fiction, and verse, Kipling enjoyed working with his hands. He was making the first permanent home he had ever known, and told editor and publisher W. E. Henley he was busy with "many things—stables and sewers and furniture. . . . It's great fun and it keeps the mind off dwelling too much on words and their texture and composition."

As never before, Rudyard was finding mental and emotional rest, though still writing many poems that he described to Henley as "a bloody flux of verse which I'm anxious to see developed." Among the poetry was a rough draft titled "In the Keddah," a poem about capturing elephants in India, "the which is a great science," he told Mary Mapes Dodge, editor of *St. Nicholas*, the popular children's magazine based in New York.

(A precursor to *The Jungle Books*, the poem was never finished, and this early draft lay unknown for a hundred years in a forgotten Kipling family safe deposit box in Brattleboro's Vermont National Bank until discovered in 1992.)

In the letter to Henley, Kipling said, "The sun and the air and the light are good in this place and have made me healthy as I never was in my life. I wish you could see the place. It's three miles from anywhere and wondrous self-contained. No one can get at you and if you don't choose to call for your mail you don't get it."

That mail had to be fetched from Brattleboro. Beatty Balestier was generally the one who daily went there for the Kipling mail, having personal business in town and at the same time getting supplies and material for Bliss Cottage and for the work on the new house site.

Rudyard often went to town with Beatty, sitting cheerfully beside him on the jouncing seat of the buckboard. A real sport when he was not befuddled or fired up by drink, Beatty was a good friend to his brother-in-law. He was four years younger than Kipling, whom he called "Kip." Rudyard soon came to depend on him for managing the new house construction and handling some of the Bliss Cottage maintenance.

Whirling at top speed down the road, Beatty's team and buckboard were always driven hard, even when the road twisted steeply down through a shady stand of evergreens called "The Pines." Arriving at the Putney Road on the river flats, Beatty turned right, heading southward along the Connecticut River, clattering too fast through a covered bridge over the West River and into Brattleboro.

Rudyard's frequent shopping visits to Main Street made him a familiar sight, although his rough workclothes and battered wide-brimmed hat dismayed those who expected to see a refined and gentlemanly English author. Unlike the posh gentry of Boston who had houses in the country and promenaded fashionably on Main Street, Kipling usually wore an old brown coat, thrown open, with knickerbockers tucked into muddy top boots. It is said that when he paid an unannounced visit to Molly Cabot's weak-sighted old mother one day, she took him for the berry man.

Kipling's hands were large and strong, with fingernails that were often unkempt. He was not graceful, but rather jerky and nervous in his movements. Usually, he kept to himself while striding along the sidewalk, head down, stoop-shouldered, and whistling tunelessly as he bustled from hardware store to post office, livery stable to Chinese laundry. He had the resolute air of a man of purpose and bluntly avoided sidewalk chatter with those he thought just wanted to hobnob.

Kipling liked genuine conversation, though, especially a good joke. He was congenial, laughing heartily and loudly when relaxing in his favorite haunt, the basement bar of the Brooks House Hotel. There he shared good lager and good cheer with the local men he was meeting, one by one. As with men all around the world these days, they usually were familiar with his work. Many, perhaps,

Main Street, Brattleboro, in the 1890s.

thought they already knew him well by what they had read of his published stories, verses, and essays.

Brattleboro was on the west bank of the south-flowing Connecticut River, a half mile wide here. In 1892 this was a sophisticated enough town, fairly close to Boston, not too far from New York by train, and well known to city people who came here as tourists, day-trippers, or to make themselves a country home. Across the river was New Hampshire, which sent its share of folk over to Brattleboro when the annual county fair was held in October, packing the town with 25,000 visitors.

Famous touring lecturers arrived regularly to speak to keen Brattleboro audiences on the most timely topics. A first-rate cornet band (reputedly the best in New England) gave weekly concerts on Main Street, and the Brattleboro Musical Society had a hundred singers taking part in rehearsals and regular concerts. There was even a sixteen-piece Philharmonic Society.

Brattleboro's Main Street was a typically broad avenue a quarter mile long with red-brick buildings decorated by contrasting stone window sills, arched or square, and facades topped by painted woodwork. The Centre Congregational Church with its pointed steeple anchored the northeast end of the street, facing the Baptist Church. At the other end of Main Street, and across Whetstone Brook, was the busy railroad depot.

Green and red awnings opened over the storefronts along the sunny side of Main Street, in the center of which was the hotel and restaurant called Brooks House. At the corner of Main and High streets, Brooks House was the most imposing commercial building in town, with its wrought-iron railings and overhanging iron balcony that shaded the sidewalk.

Diagonally opposite Brooks House, on the east side of the street, was the 1855 Brattleboro Town Hall, where Town Clerk and Justice of the Peace William S. Newton had his office. Talk was of soon renovating the town hall, which also held the post office on the ground floor with a meeting room for selectmen beside the clerk's office. The actual hall for town meetings and public lectures was on the second floor, where court cases requiring extra space were heard.

Behind the buildings on the east side of Main Street ran the embankment for the Boston and Maine Railroad, just above the river.

When the Kiplings first returned from their wedding journey in August, Brattleboro's temperature was more than a hundred degrees. "Men—hatless, coatless and gasping—lay in the shade of that station where only a few months ago the glass stood at 30 below zero."

To Rudyard, it appeared that Main Street in blazing summertime "had given up the business of life, and an American flag with some politician's name printed across the bottom hung down across the street stiff as a board. There were men with fans and alpaca coats curled up in splint chairs in the verandah of the one hotel—among them an ex-President of the United States. He completed the impression that the furniture of the entire country had been turned out of doors for summer cleaning. . . ."

Brooks House had seen better days when the spas were flourishing, but in 1892 there was still plenty of business and an occasional ex-president as guest to keep the former manager, "Colonel" Francis Goodhue II, busy with local gossip. In the Brooks House basement was a tavern with a billiards table, and here Col. Goodhue often could be found chatting with customers, who ranged from the likes of Rudyard and Beatty to lawyers, shopkeepers, tourists, schoolteachers, and farmers—and of course that former president (probably Rutherford B. Hayes).

Kipling preferred the Vermont country to the town. He liked the farmers best, describing them as "unhandy men to cross in their ways, set, silent, indirect in speech. . . ." He said, "They are not much heard in the streets" or in the city papers, and outsiders seldom take them into account when judging America, but "*they* are the American."

From the stoop of Bliss Cottage Kipling greeted farmhands swinging by on their way home from the fields in the evening, and he thought of their mowing machines standing silent in the meadow: ". . . and the horses are shaking themselves. The last of the sunlight leaves the top of Monadnock, and four miles away Main Street lights her electric lamps. It is band night in Main Street, and the folks from Putney, from Marlboro', from Guilford, and even New Fane will drive in their well-filled waggons to hear music and to look at the Ex-President."

The Brattleboro Congregational minister, Rev. Charles O. Day, first saw Kipling while they were both dining at Brooks House: ". . . though I recognized him from portraits which I had seen, I might have done so from the constant play of comment from him as his eye fell on every little object in the room with the liveliest curiosity."

In remembrance years later, Rev. Day said "Mr. Kipling was most generous in his gift of entertainment; his conversation was precisely like his books at their best, and touched upon a wide range of subjects. . . . He would talk interestingly, clearly, brilliantly upon such topics as classes in English society, the amusements of remote rajahs in India, English newspapers and periodicals . . . American politics. . . ."

For all that Kipling was cheerful and full of fun when talking with friends and those he respected, he liked to stand back, listen, and observe whenever he could. He was determined to learn about Americans firsthand in order to write about them authentically. He sought to deepen his knowledge of the people and culture and to use the result in stories and verse. He always carried folded writing paper and a pencil in his pocket, pausing now and again to make notes, catching quotations or expressions or characteristics he wanted to remember.

Kipling's own eccentric mannerisms left a lasting impression, particularly his awkward, almost rude standoffishness that could alternate with an eager, prying curiosity about all he saw. There were times when Kipling would sit in the Brattleboro train station for hours, talking with stationmaster Dave Carey about the movements and mechanics of trains, or chatting with travelers coming and going.

Often, he sat in the background at the station, observing and listening, usually smoking a cheroot or puffing on a black briar pipe—the latter described by an American hostess in 1889 as "perfectly villainous."

For the first few weeks after moving into Bliss Cottage on August 10th, the Kiplings were kept busy with the mundane necessities of creating their home, painting woodwork, making a space for writing, and putting up bedsteads.

Rudyard enjoyed lingering in the Brattleboro train station, where he chatted with the stationmaster while studying American travelers and listening to their manners of speech.

The white clapboard Bliss Cottage had eight rooms, was a story and a half high, seventeen feet long, and including the kitchen and woodshed was twenty-seven feet wide. It had a "deep if dampish cellar," said Rudyard, in which they installed a huge, secondhand hot-air woodstove.

"We cut generous holes in our thin floors for its eight-inch pipes (why we were never burned in our beds each week of the winter I can never understand) and we were extraordinarily and self-centredly content."

Although in those first weeks Kipling was undisturbed by the outside press, he soon had a request from Frederick Childs, the Brattleboro postmaster, who wanted to interview him for the *Springfield Republican,* for which Childs was a special correspondent.

Kipling wrote in reply: "I'm sorry I'm not able to help you in the matter referred to in your note of yesterday's date but it is my rule never to supply newspapers with any information whatever. This saves my time, which is valuable to me, stimulates their imagination which is wonderful, and does no harm to anybody. I have not broken that rule yet and America is a bad place to begin in. Again, I am very sorry not to be able to meet you here, for it would have been of service to you—but business is business, and mine, you understand, is keeping still."

Childs did not again attempt to interview Kipling, and they remained friendly acquaintances.

During the next weeks, as "the New England summer flamed into autumn," Kipling "piled cut spruce boughs all round the draughty cottage sill, and helped to put up a tiny roofless verandah along one side of it for future needs."

In early October, his remote privacy came somewhat undone upon the death of the British poet laureate, Alfred Lord Tennyson, as rumor spread that Rudyard was a likely choice to replace him. Although it was at first kept secret, Kipling was discreetly "sounded on the subject" by friends of government officials. He politely declined, however, even to be considered as the next poet laureate. It was a position of great honor, yet one which required its holder to write to order on state occasions and upon subjects selected by the monarch and Parliament.

Highly placed political friends of Kipling thought he should be the foremost candidate because of his influential "public poems" such as "The Ballad of East and West" and "The English Flag." Learning he might be formally proposed for the office of poet laureate, Kipling told his friends in the government that he would be of more value to the empire if he were free to write what he chose. He did not want to embarrass the queen with a flat, public refusal of the laureateship, but made it plain he would never write flowery odes to the political moment or to commemorate royal birthdays.

As for Parliament in 1892, it was controlled by the Liberal party and Prime Minister W. E. Gladstone, whom Kipling had more than once contemptuously criticized. Gladstone, in fact, would not likely have conferred the laureateship on Kipling, the gadfly conservative, but there was much speculation about it in those days, even in the States.

That October, Kipling later recalled, "Reporters came from papers in Boston, which I presume believed itself to be civilised, and demanded interviews. I told them I had nothing to say. 'If ye heven't, guess we'll *make* ye say something.' So they went away and lied copiously, their orders being to 'get the story.'"

Carrie Kipling's diary said that unwanted visit of the reporters "wrecked" the day for them. The so-called interviews appeared late that month in the *Boston Herald* and *Boston Globe.*

"The days go peacefully, each with its stint and the Peace of God upon each," Kipling wrote to W. E. Henley, also telling about his encounters with the snooping press. "Now and again I have to explain the shortest way back again to a wandering reporter who tells me with tears in his eyes that he is a gentleman and

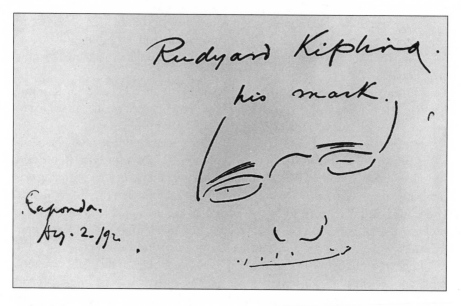

A sketch by Kipling, made on August 2, 1892, while he was on an outing to Lake Raponda, near Wilmington, Vermont, west of Brattleboro.

proceeds to prove it by trying to get the village . . . tailor to show him my clothes. Otherwise I am deliciously alone. . . ."

By now he was helping Beatty with the site preparation for Naulakha high on the hillside. The house would look right at the tip of Monadnock beyond the Chesterfield hills. He told Henley he was learning "to master the science (I think it's a calling) of ox-driving. O Henley, papers are easier to edit than oxen, a yoke of 'em, are to drive. They drained me dry of profanity yesterday in the woods."

He and Carrie were getting ready for the winter and for the coming of a baby. Working hard physically, Kipling was perhaps truly happy for the first time in his life. As a boy he had been miserable when, for five long years until age eleven, he had been placed with foster parents while attending primary school. Then, as a near-sighted, unathletic lad in a cold and spartan private school for future army officers and civil servants, he had made his way quite successfully and was recognized as a leader by the time he was almost seventeen.

After that, Kipling returned to India to work "seven years hard" as a newspaper reporter, contending with fever, stifling heat, and class-conscious British bureaucrats whose society was even more stratified than the Indian caste system.

Having traveled around the world, making journey upon journey and never finding rest, Rudyard had discovered a new beginning in beautiful Vermont. Life was full of promise and hope, and there was a real home in his future.

"Never you mind about my living in America," he told Henley. "If you saw this life of ours and didn't happen to know your geography, it would be Africa, or Australia or another planet. I have what I need. Sunshine and a mind at ease, peace and my own time for my own work and the real earth within the reach of my hand, whenever I tire of messing with ink. Good stuff will come out of this in God's time which is not my time; and if nothing comes, then I shall have led a sane clean life at least, and found new experiences."

Winter in America—
All the flowers go—
All except Sweet Marjorie
Blooming in the snow.

Untitled, 1892

Chapter 5

The Stillness of Winter

Life was not, however, all physical labor and detached observation of Vermont manners. Kipling was thinking about the first *Jungle Book* story, "Toomai of the Elephants," to be published by *St. Nicholas*. He wrote to editor, Mary Mapes Dodge: "Now if that tale pleases you, I will do 'Tiger-Tiger'—the tale of the man eater who was ignominiously squelched in his lair by the charge of the village buffaloes under the command of the little boy herd. That's a true tale.

"Also, there will be (*D. V.*) a wolf tale, 'Mowgli's Brothers.' *He* was a wolf boy (we have them in India) but being caught early was civilized." He then suggested a camel story: "It will be a regular Zoo," adding that there ought to be a title for them: "Noah's Ark tales? or how?"

These "Noah's Ark" tales were at the fore of Kipling's thoughts by Thanksgiving, which was spent, according to Rev. Day, at "the home of a dear friend of his wife and her family." Perhaps this friend was Molly Cabot.

Rev. Day wrote about that Thanksgiving: "I recall his vivid description, given for the benefit of children present, of the doings of the troops of monkeys—the too familiar inhabitants of the gardens and even dwellings of his Indian homes. The style of *The Jungle Books*, which had not then seen the light, was in the storytelling." In the delighting of children Kipling found special joy, and he could entertain them for hours with stories and verses made up on the spot. He told Rev. Day, "He who could reach the child's heart could reach the world's heart."

St. Nick's Mary Mapes Dodge could have no inkling, as yet, of the lasting power of the stories she was commissioning from the prolific young Rudyard Kipling. Many other magazines and publishers were also after him, his work appearing in *Scribners, Harper's, McClure's*, and the *Ladies' Home Journal* as well as in a number of newspapers, including the *Civil and Military Gazette* of India, which originally published him in the days when he was a struggling reporter. Now, he was extremely well paid, his rates being $100 per 1,000 words in a time when several hundred dollars a year was a good wage.

Though for the past few months Kipling's literary output had been small compared to the previous two years of explosive production and sudden fame, his financial loss in the bank failure that spring was more than recouped during his first half-year in Vermont. Royalties from *The Naulahka* and *Barrack-room Ballads* were coming in: $150 in September, $260 in October, and then an astonishing $3,888 in November. This was just the beginning.

With his work in great demand, and everything he wrote saleable for top dollar, Kipling was cautious not to fall back into the habit of strenuous overwork and nervous exhaustion that in the past had led to illness. Now it was his practice to have several pieces in progress at the same time. These generally differed from one another—a ballad, a serious story, a lighter piece, verse—and in this way he could turn from one to the other in accord with his moods. He often laid unfinished work aside, perhaps for brief reflection, sometimes for months.

Since the mid-eighties, Kipling had been developing a long tale of India that followed the adventures of a street waif with English blood who joins up with a mystical Tibetan lama. He wrote about this story to Mary Mapes Dodge, telling of the boy's adventures as the lama searches for "a miraculous river that washed away all sin . . . and how these two went hunting for it together. . . ."

This was the foundation of *Kim,* the novel said to be Kipling's greatest creation. First, however, would come the "Noah's Ark Tales" of Indian jungle creatures and Mowgli, the wolf-boy raised among them.

Kipling prepared for his first New England winter and for the baby. His child and the jungle creatures would be born at Bliss Cottage, in "the big silence of the snow."

As the weather turned cold, Kipling wrote to family back in England: "I am very busy and very happy up here among the hills. The winter snows have not come yet but we expect them so to speak every minute and sleighs and snow shoes are being got ready with the fur coats and rugs. We two are also waiting for another arrival. He is expected late next month or early in January. . . . He'll be a snow baby but I hope none the worse on that account."

Carrie's mother, Anna, and sister, Josephine, came to stay at Bliss Cottage that Christmas, prepared to help when the baby arrived. Still there had been no real snow. Kipling was invigorated by the crisp climate, which contrasted with the gloom-and-fog winter of England:

"Here we become angry at an overcast day and accept God's light as though it were in the nature of things—as indeed I am beginning to believe that it is. The special beauty of the weather is that one can work largely, longly and continuously and the burden of the work evaporates in the sunshine so that a man can do much and yet not feel that he is doing anything."

It was customary for Kipling to write all morning, until one in the afternoon. Then the cottage was kept silent, disturbed only when he called to Carrie in frustration for help finding the right word or rhyme. Visitors were not welcome in this time, and as usual it was Carrie who kept the world at bay.

Luncheon was a cheerful meal, sometimes with guests, but even in little Bliss Cottage, dinner was at eight, with husband and wife dressing for it. After a bachelor's catch-as-catch-can life of missed meals and greasy-spoon eateries, Kipling was not overly enthusiastic about formal dinners, but he went along to please Carrie, perpetuating her family's French traditions. She said one reason to dress for dinner was to keep the respect of their servants.

Kipling grumbled about formal dinners to John Bliss, a fellow his own age and owner of the rented cottage. "When your work is over you can go into the kitchen and have supper. I have to dress up in evening clothes."

Beatty's friend, Frederic Van de Water, wrote, perhaps exaggeratedly, about what he had heard of those months, saying the "enigmas" of the household "chronically bewildered" their Swedish maid, Anna Anderson:

"How, Anna wondered, could a man sit at a desk all day, smoking and writing with equal fury? Why should a wife be so indignant if her husband's apparently trivial task were disturbed? And why—by all the customs of Sweden, why, should a man and wife, alone in a snow-lapped cottage, miles from the nearest town, appear at their small table, each night, at dinner time, arrayed in full evening dress—Kipling in white tie and tails; his wife in a low cut gown with train?"

White tie? A gown with train?

John Bliss was a guest at a number of dinners and dropped in now and again when the Kiplings were at table. He confirmed they had formal dinners, company or not, but "I can't remember that his wife did wear evening dress every night. I rather think she did not."

Kipling accepted Carrie's mannered ways, and she became more and more the force that guided his business and social matters. Their marriage was a perfect blend of personalities for a creative writer who needed definite working hours as well as someone to manage his affairs. Kipling could throw himself into work, while Carrie took charge of everyday business, including keeping the accounts and paying Beatty for work on the house site. She watched every cent and demanded receipts for everything. Carrie paid her brother in both very small and very large amounts, and he had to come to her for his cash. This naturally placed him at his sister's beck and call.

Beatty started well, and the project went smoothly, so that before the snow was too deep, everything was ready for the builders to begin in the spring. The situation was good, and the two families got along. The vivacious and beautiful Mai Mendon Balestier loved a large party, and the Kiplings were invited to Maplewood for gatherings that were full of fun, music, and hearty country life. Their first Vermont Christmas was at Beatty's home.

Biographer Carrington described the parties: "With cakes on a plank table, jugs of home-brewed cider, a fiddler from the town; with all the neighbors in they would dance in the barn till past midnight—ungodly hours for Brattleboro."

And more than once, Rudyard stood amongst the delighted guests to extemporize verse after verse, usually humorous, tapping rhythms on a table with one hand and even sketching accompanying pictures on paper as he went. At one party, Molly Cabot heard him spontaneously recite seventy-five verses without pause. Rudyard showed his affection for Mai and Beatty by composing a poem for little Marjorie. It was never published but was preserved as a Balestier keepsake years afterwards.

Winter in America—
All the flowers go—
All except Sweet Marjorie
Blooming in the snow.

Snow upon the window sill.
Frost upon the pane.
Baby wakes & winks & then
Goes to sleep again.

Winter comes across the field
And the snowdrift flies—
Trouble in America
Baby wakes & cries.

Oh the white wreath in the hedge!
Little Baby cares
When she hears her mother bring
Dinner up the stairs.

What care we for driving wind,
  Snow or winter's wrath?—
Cyclones in America
  Baby's in her bath.

Twilight falls across the snow;
  Windows glimmer red—
Silence in America
  Baby goes to bed.

Kipling signed it "Rud (Poet Laureate to Marjorie) escripit."

Winter was difficult in Vermont, but that first one was an adventure for Rudyard at the isolated cottage. "Sometimes we would have a servant. Sometimes she would find the solitude too much for her and flee without warning. . . .

"When our lead pipe froze, we would slip on our coon-skin coats and thaw it out with a lighted candle. There was no space in the attic bedroom for a cradle, so we decided that a trunk tray would be just as good. We envied no one—not even when skunks wandered into our cellar and, knowing the nature of the beasts, we immobilised ourselves till it should please them to depart."

Then came the first deep snow, and with it their child, born on December 29th, precisely before their own birthdays, the 30th and 31st. When Carrie went into labor, Kipling rushed to the home of John Bliss, asking him to fetch Dr. James Conland, who came to deliver a girl—named Josephine, for Carrie's sister and for Rudyard, whose first name was Joseph. They were overjoyed.

With typical English understatement, Kipling reined in his joy when he wrote to Henley a few days later: "Now everything is happily over—but I do wish she hadn't had the bad taste to be born on Gladstone's birthday. That reconciles me to her being a girl. If she had been a boy 'twould have been my duty to stand her on her head in a drift lest she also should disgrace the empire.

"You can guess how happy we are: all things are going so excellently. Her chin is mine and the rest is dough but there's no doubt about the chin. Nor un-luckily about the temper which is anything but civilized."

Kipling later wrote of baby Josephine that "she throve in her trunk-tray in the sunshine on the little plank verandah. Her birth brought me into contact with the best friend I made in New England—Dr. Conland."

About fourteen years older than Kipling, James Conland was also an outsider in Brattleboro, having been born in New York City and raised as an orphan on

Cape Cod. Conland was a strong, fine-looking figure, known for visiting the back farms in a hooded sleigh in all kinds of weather, seldom wearing an overcoat. It was a comfort to the Kiplings to have him as a close family friend and physician; he and Rudyard were often found together at the Brooks House bar.

"When winter shut down and sleigh-bells rang all over the white world that tucked us in, we counted ourselves secure," Kipling wrote of the days after the baby was born. He took pleasure in the daily routine of country life, far from the writers' garrets, stylish salons, and slushy streets of London. He enjoyed rolling out the snowbound roads with teams of oxen in company with John Bliss. Kipling, said Bliss, did not have the skill to drive the oxen, but liked to touch them lightly with the whip.

After a storm, Kipling wrote, "The farmers shovel a way to their beasts, bind with chains their large ploughshares to their heaviest wood-sled and take of oxen as many as Allah has given them. These they drive, and the dragging share makes a furrow in which a horse can walk, and the oxen, by force of repeatedly going in up to their bellies, presently find foothold. The finished road is a deep double gutter between three-foot walls of snow, where, by custom, the heavier vehicle has the right of way. The lighter man when he turns out must drop waist-deep and haul his unwilling beast into the drift, leaving Providence to steady the sleigh."

Kipling's workroom in the Bliss Cottage was just seven by eight feet, and in December the snow came to lie "level with its windowsill." He sat at his desk and thought about life in India and the creatures of the jungle and about the tale he had written years ago, "which included a boy who had been brought up by wolves.

"In the stillness, and suspense, of the winter . . . some memory of the Masonic Lions of my childhood's magazine, and a phrase in Haggard's *Nada the Lily*, combined with the echo of this tale. After blocking out the main idea in my head, the pen took charge, and I watched it begin to write stories about Mowgli and animals, which later grew into *The Jungle Books*.

"Two tales, I remember, I threw away and was better pleased with the remainder. More to the point, my Father thought well of the workmanship."

As with all fables, there is inevitably a moral behind his *Jungle Books* stories. Kipling, himself, conceded his writing usually had a double meaning or a moral beneath the surface.

He told British editor W. E. Henley, "I've been neglecting prose for verse and besides I've struck a vein of animal yarns that is leading me further afield than I thought."

Mowgli, the human outsider who must find his place in the wild jungle, was created by a man who, himself, did not wholly belong anywhere, and who had to discover his own true nature. For years Kipling had been one of the English handful in the vast native population of India. Then he had been a colonial Anglo-Indian back in "street-bred" England. Later he had bucked the British literary establishment with his swift, sometimes vulgar stories and slashing wit.

Success had propelled him to the fore as an influential young upstart who did not have the proper schooling and refined bloodlines essential for acceptance into the British ruling class—though many of them were avid Kipling readers. Now, in America, he was more than ever an outsider.

As an Englishman with intense patriotism and burning ideals regarding the responsibility of white (specifically Anglo-Saxon) men, he was uncomfortable in a giant (mainly Anglo-Saxon) country that avoided international responsibility while it accused the English of being no more than rapacious empire-builders.

The knee-jerk, anti-imperial attitude of many Americans troubled Kipling, for he believed the developed industrial nations were morally obliged to modernize and educate the backward lands. By so doing, developed nations would free benighted people from tyrants and superstition. Guidance had to come from the enlightened—and conveniently well-armed—modern nations, though it cost dearly in the sweat and blood of thousands of young idealists who went out on humanitarian missions with no expectation of personal glory or recompense.

From his years in teeming India, Kipling knew plenty of young British idealists who had died, exhausted and broken, while striving to improve the lot of the natives. Few Americans, however, with their inborn hatred of empires, could take the idealism of an imperialist seriously.

Kipling cloaked his opinions of right and wrong in these semi-fables, these children's tales called *The Jungle Books*. Just as there was a natural "Law of the Jungle," as Kipling coined the term, so was there a natural law governing humanity and all nations. As with the creatures of Kipling's fabulous jungle, those peoples and nations who lived "without the Law" faced grave consequences.

And just as Mowgli of *The Jungle Books* must find his true identity while confronted by the forces described in the poem "Law of the Jungle," so must Kipling find his own identity, his own life's purpose. In the 1890s the world seemed ever on the edge of war. Astonishing scientific and technological progress, advanced communications, and devastating new weaponry combined with colonial unrest and an international web of espionage to make the real world more dangerous than any imaginary jungle.

For now, though, Rudyard was caught up in this winter-bound little world in the Vermont hills. Awestruck by the temperatures dropping from forty degrees on a sunny afternoon to minus thirty by the next morning, he made the best of it, and with buoyant spirits. Rudyard especially loved to snowshoe through the woods with Beatty or Will Cabot or John Bliss, and took to the thrill of riding a home-made sled down the icy slopes— "a box on a board and perhaps the most danger-ous business you could well get into. There is absolutely no finality to a slide down hill until you hit a stone wall."

I have made for you a song,
*   And it may be right or wrong,*
But only you can tell me if it's true;
*   I have tried for to explain*
*   Both your pleasure and your pain,*
And, Thomas, here's my best respects to you!

*   O there'll surely come a day*
*   When they'll give you all your pay,*
And treat you as a Christian ought to do;
*   So, until that day comes round,*
*   Heaven keep you safe and sound,*
And, Thomas, here's my best respects to you!

To Thomas Atkins
Prelude to *Barrack-room Ballads*, 1892

Chapter 6

Fame, Family, and Life in a Fairy Tale

The Mowgli stories were a drastic change from the hard-edged, indiscreet close-ups of British life that had brought Kipling fame and fortune. Until now, most of his poems, stories, and essays had been about the ordinary human condition, seldom written about so well before. Heedless of the resentment he might stir up, Kipling had spoken his mind vigorously, sometimes too brashly and too precisely, too full of the self-righteousness of youth.

Fascinated by those who sparked his curiosity, Kipling was distant and aloof with those he did not like. He was particularly repelled by effete literary and art critics, and in 1890 wrote the verses "In Partibus," declaring that he hated to

> *. . . consort with long-haired things*
> *In velvet collar rolls,*
>
> *Who talk about the Aims of Art,*
> *And 'theories' and 'goals',*
> *And moo and coo with womenfolk*
> *About their blessed souls.*

Thus did he describe the likes of Oscar Wilde, then in London and known to Kipling. Kipling repelled them in turn with his rowdy verse and stage cockney, his raw emotions and ironic humor. He preferred the company of soldiers and workmen in the smoky, noisy music halls. The underclass adored Kipling, because he spoke for them, and the whole empire read what he said.

> *It's Oh to meet an Army man,*
> *Set up and trimmed and taut,*
> *Who does not spout hashed libraries*
> *Or think the next man's thought,*
> *And walks as though he owned himself,*
> *And hogs his bristles short.*

By the time he settled down in Vermont, Kipling had mellowed somewhat, tempered by experience and gentled by a happy marriage and life in a quiet place. He still intended to speak his mind, of course, and believed what he had to say to the world was important.

Kipling saw himself in primitive terms as a tribal singer, much like the imaginary spell-weavers and chanters of prehistoric times, the conscience and voice of a folk's soul. In winter at Bliss Cottage he expressed this with the satirical "In the Neolithic Age":

> *In the Neolithic Age savage warfare did I wage*
> *For food and fame and wooly horses' pelt;*
> *I was singer to my clan in that dim, red Dawn of Man,*
> *And I sang of all we fought and feared and felt.*

When the tribal singer is criticized by a rival:

> *'Neath my tomahawk of diorite he fell.*
> *And I left my views on Art, barbed and tanged, below the heart*
> *Of a mammothistic etcher at Grenelle.*

The singer declares, "For I know my work is right and theirs was wrong." But the spirits of the totem shame the singer, and tell him:

> *"There are nine and sixty ways of constructing tribal lays,*
> *"And every single one of them is right."*

Reincarnated "beneath Time's finger, once again a tribal singer," the poet now views the world and art more wisely and more tolerantly.

> *Here's my wisdom for your use, as I learned it when the moose*
> *And the reindeer roared where Paris roars to-night:—*
> "There are nine and sixty ways of constructing tribal lays,
> "And–every–single–one–of–them–is–right!"

In his seclusion at Bliss Cottage that winter of 1892–93, Kipling reflected on his years in India and on his globe-trotting.

He wrote "Song of the Cities," impressions of the British empire seaports he had visited, from Bombay to Singapore, Hong Kong to Quebec. He also wrote new verses about the life of soldiers in the British Indian Army, but his mind was more than ever on the Mowgli stories. He thought about these "beast tales" as he took long afternoon walks on snowshoes, or meditated in his study. Only the crying of the baby broke the morning silence, and that sound the proud father did not much mind.

Kipling loved his new life, but could not quite understand his Vermont neighbors. He did not like their inquisitiveness, no matter that it was an expression of typical American friendliness. He was not used to the culture, and at first wanted nothing to do with that part of it. He was an outsider and felt, rightly or wrongly, that many folk here did not take to him.

In his autobiography four decades later, he wrote: "Here was a stranger of an unloved race, currently reported to 'make as much as a hundred dollars out of a ten-cent bottle of ink,' and who had 'pieces in the papers' about him, who had married a 'Balestier girl.' Did not her grandmother still live on the Balestier place, where 'old Balestier' instead of farming had built a rather large house, and there had dined late in special raiment, and drunk red wines after the custom of the French instead of decent whisky? And behold this Britisher, under pretext of having lost money, had settled this wife down 'right among her own folk' in the Bliss Cottage. It was not seemly on the face of it; so they watched as secretively as the New England or English peasant can, and what toleration they extended to the 'Britisher' was solely for the sake of 'the Balestier girl.' "

In 1892 Rudyard Kipling's reputation was already great, and he was considered one of the finest prose writers of the day. With the publication that year of the collection of poems entitled *Barrack-room Ballads*, his fame was redoubled.

These verses were rough and ready, never-before-seen close-ups of "Tommy Atkins," the lowly British soldier who was until then almost invisible to the general population except in time of war. (Thomas Atkins was the fictitious soldier's name used on sample paperwork and forms in the British Army.)

Kipling's soldier expressed his sense of being an outcast in the poem "Tommy":

> *I went into a public-'ouse to get a pint o' beer,*
> *The publican 'e up an' sez, "We serve no red-coats here."*
> *The girls be'ind the bar they laughed and giggled fit to die,*
> *I outs into the street again an' to myself sez I:*
> *O it's Tommy this an' Tommy that, an' "Tommy, go away";*
> *But it's "Thank you, Mr. Atkins," when the band begins to play—*

Soldiers were indeed outcasts, considered the dregs of society, harshly disciplined, poorly paid, and utterly unwanted until the country went to war—as Kipling's Tommy Atkins drily puts it, "when the band begins to play."

The poems were electric, exciting, alive with right-on character and color, and widely controversial, for speaking well of hard-case soldiers was unthinkable among those British who thought themselves to be the better sort. Until then, no important writer had risked being identified with the cause of the common soldier the way Kipling did.

Barrack-room Ballads such as "Tommy" and "Danny Deever" portrayed the tough soldiers as human beings, and these characters even expressed their opinions of commanders. The famous field marshal Lord Roberts—whom Kipling knew—was known to the men affectionately as "Bobs," the title of a Kipling poem to him.

Kipling's soldiers spoke of their native counterparts across the battlefield with a respect that startled and moved civilian readers: "Fuzzy-Wuzzy" was the nickname the troops used for the Sudanese fighters defeated not long before by a British expeditionary force.

> *We've fought with many men acrost the seas,*
> *An' some of 'em was brave and some was not:*
> *The Pathan an' the Zulu an' Burmese;*
> *But the Fuzzy was the finest o' the lot.*
>
> * * *
>
> *So 'ere's to you, Fuzzy-Wuzzy, at your 'ome in the Soudan;*
> *You're a pore benighted 'eathen, but a first-class fightin' man;*

Kipling speaks with the voice of the soldier who matter-of-factly does his duty, with no boasting, and with the understatement of a real hero.

> *Then 'ere's to you, Fuzzy-Wuzzy, an' the missis and the kid;*
> *Our orders was to break you, an' of course we went an' did.*

Millions in the empire and America thrilled to these unvarnished, gritty characterizations of the men who fought and won the wars. The verses were full of Tommy's laconic humor, and sometimes bitterness while he resolutely accepted the fighting man's lot.

Both British and American soldiers liked Kipling, as did foreign soldiers who read him in translation (especially the French). The rollicking English music halls and the American variety shows and saloons echoed with Rudyard's poems, often recited from the stage, and many were set to music.

His love of India, and his respect for the native people he knew there, first as a child and later as a young man, pours out in one of his most famous poems, "Gunga Din." A humble Hindu regimental water-carrier who "never seemed to know the use of fear" is portrayed as the finest of "them black-faced crew" serving the British troops under fire.

But Kipling's Gunga Din is far more than just an admirable native: he is looked upon by the otherwise callous Tommy Atkins in a way that even idealistic British missionaries and bleeding heart social-reformers could scarcely imagine in those days:

> *Though I've belted you and flayed you,*
> *By the livin' Gawd that made you,*
> *You're a better man than I am, Gunga Din!*

Through that first Vermont winter of 1892–93, Kipling enjoyed unsurpassed international admiration. Soon there would be a sudden flow of money from the best-selling *Barrack-room Ballads*. Not since the British poet Lord Byron had any writer achieved such great success so rapidly.

Letters of praise and inquiry poured into the Brattleboro post office from around the world, a hundred or more every day. It was impossible to answer them all. The Kiplings set a policy that Rudyard would not without good reason answer any letters from unknown admirers or seekers of his literary advice or autograph. The letters were read by Carrie each day and most thrown away. (Kipling did, however, keep for his personal use any return stamps sent by unknown hopefuls who wanted him to reply.)

On the other hand, Kipling always responded generously to a friend's manuscript, giving no-nonsense advice. Often, he would tell the writer that his fee "for a written opinion, suggestions, etc." was five dollars, which should be sent as a donation to the Fresh Air Fund in New York, one of his favorite charities.

As months passed, the Kiplings delighted in watching the growth of their first-born, Josephine—sometimes called Jo or Joss, a pidgin-English term for a Chinese religious statue. Kipling wrote to a cousin, "Joss suits her better now seeing as she is the image of a Burmese idol and I'm afraid The Joss she'll remain till late in life.

"Carrie is walking through new worlds, wild with happiness and though I can't pretend to know The Joss intimately or to talk to her she is more than very dear to me." Kipling's letters are full of his affection for Josephine: ". . . there's no disguising it—the sweetest infant in all the world." He already felt protective of her, finding it hard to imagine sending Josephine to school in her first eight years. He wrote to England, saying it would be "like walking in dreams" to bring his own child over to meet his cousin's children.

The Kiplings hired an English nurse for the baby. "No good to defile her speech at the very outset with the Yank peacock cry!"

He wrote that Josephine "lived" on a pillow, watching him as he worked in his study. For now, she slept in the trunk tray, but in the new house there would be "a little brass crib and a day and a night nursery and everything handsome about her." She would not be an only child out here in the country, he said, because "Babie Marjorie my brother in law's child is here to take care of her or kill her. I don't know which. Her love for the baby is very touching. She brings it everything from old shoes to the waste paper basket, crooning with delight all the while."

Into this letter crept disapproval of how the careless Beatty was raising his own daughter. "Marjorie is really a radiantly beautiful baby and if she does not get kicked to death in the stables, or gored or stung or anything she will be a lovely woman."

The Kiplings experienced the common and dangerous hazards of the Vermont winter. One day the dependable black horse Marcus Aurelius lost his footing and slid down an icy slope "sitting on his tail till the sparks flew," dragging the sleigh with the frightened Kiplings aboard. But for all the ice and fierce blasts of cold wind, they delighted in their simple life and in the privacy of Bliss Cottage. ·

When any writing was ready, Carrie was Rudyard's first audience. They sat by the stove, she listening as Rudyard, usually wearing a fez, read his verse or stories aloud. Being nearsighted, he pushed his glasses up onto his forehead and brought the paper close to his face. When silently reading books, Kipling's eyes quickly scanned the page, his fingers slipping between two or three next pages, which he turned rapidly. Ever since his youth, onlookers thought Kipling could not possibly be getting anything out of what he was reading, but he insisted he did not miss anything that mattered.

Without his glasses, Kipling was virtually blind at any distance. A friend from his days at the United Services College—a boys' prep school at the seacoast hamlet of Westward Ho! in Devon, England—described his eyes without the glasses as "strange, vibrating and blind, only seeing clearly a matter of inches." As the sole student in that school wearing glasses (few boys did in those days), he earned the nickname "Gigger," or "Giglamps," because his thick lenses resembled carriage lamps.

In his seven years working in India, Kipling had been very close to his parents and sister, Trix—"The Family Square," they called it. Now he had his American family to care about him and his work. The Kiplings visited Carrie's grandmother, Madam Balestier, at Beechwood, to show off the baby and to read Rudyard's latest work to her. Beatty and Mai also generally were told when a piece was finished and ready to be sent to a periodical or a book publisher.

For the first time in his life, Kipling felt truly at home somewhere. He had loved Bombay, the city of his birth and early years, but once uprooted he had never gone back to live there. Lahore and Allahabad had been little more than living quarters while he worked twelve hours a day on the newspapers and developed his skills. Nor had London been home to him, with its island-bound laboring classes and snobbish intellectuals who could not understand the Anglo-Indian. In all his thousands of miles traveling around the world, Kipling was not only at home here, in Vermont, but he was healthier than ever.

He wrote happily to England about that first snowbound winter: "I wonder if you can realize weather that only goes above freezing for half an hour at midday sometimes: and yet is dancing, clear, dry buoyant weather. . . . There is neither dust nor smoke nor defilement of any kind."

For a man with lungs that suffered in the bone-chilling, smoky English damp, Kipling began to feel stronger with each passing week and often spent hours walking or working outside.

"The trees are Emperors with their crowns on and icicles five and six feet long hang from our eaves. It's all like life in a fairy tale—life when one sings and shouts for joy of being alive. . . ."

The Kiplings had four oxen to haul firewood and break roads, and when the way was clear, Rudyard and the family went to town and back on a new "great roomy wicker Maryland sleigh" drawn by Marcus Aurelius. When they got out of the sleigh, the horse would lie down in the traces and fall asleep until they returned.

Kipling, this Anglo-Indian not so long away from the unforgettable blistering heat of India, described their "life running on sleighs" as the "trees groan in the frost," adding that although it might sound oppressive, "I can only say that I've never been cold yet as I've been cold in London and I have never had to put a wrap about my throat: neither have I had a cold or a cough since August last."

Back in the fall, he had moments when he still thought longingly of that unfinished journey to the balmy South Seas, but even then it was with a sense of humor, and not true disappointment. American author Charles Warren Stoddard sent a copy of his book *South-Sea Idylls*, published by Scribners in 1892, and Kipling replied in a letter that it was not "quite kind of you to send it. I'm settled down for a New England winter, in a grey land among an austere people two hundred miles from the water. . . ."

Stoddard's book gave Kipling "as bad an attack of 'go-fever' as I've had for a long time past." A year earlier, he had recovered from the disappointment of not going on to those islands, "but you've stirred me up again."

He signed the letter to Stoddard, "Yours hungrily, admiringly and upsettedly," but it was tongue-in-cheek. With the making of a home in the cottage and the birth of the baby, Kipling was content. The promise of a house of his own was further satisfying to him through the harsh New England winter and into the thawing weeks of mud season.

In March he wrote to author and poet James Whitcomb Riley of Indiana, thanking him for a copy of *Green Fields and Running Brooks,* Riley's latest book. They admired each other's work, Kipling saying his profound emotional response to Riley's best poems made it certain "there is a poet at the keyboard."

Rikki-tikki-tavi confronts Nag the cobra in *The Jungle Books*. Illustrator: W.H. Drake

Lord, send a man like Robbie Burns to sing the Song o' Steam!

McAndrew's Hymn, 1893

Chapter 7

'Barbarism Plus Telephone: I Like It'

Kipling had relatively little to do with the people of Brattleboro. Still, he clucked disapprovingly in a letter to Baltimore writer Edward Lucas White, saying "God knows why—they are yearning to defile their pretty town with a trolley. Not street cars . . . but a sizzling electric outfit in order that they may keep up with the procession."

He said, "Except to buy things we have no dealings with the aborigines. Nobody comes to interrupt; nobody wants to see me and I can work as long as ever I please and yet have time to be out for three or four hours a day."

For all that he did not have much direct contact with the Americans around him, Kipling was learning about them. He wrote to Henley expressing surprise that "in this back of beyond" there would be a lecture by Paul Belloni Du Chaillu, a famous African explorer and writer.

". . . and I'm going down to listen to him and see how the aborigines take it. Me and the aborigines are excellent friends but they can't understand why I don't come to chicken suppers and church sociables and turkey sprees."

He went on to say Charles Dickens "never did better work" than in his *American Notes*, which were harshly critical about the United States at mid-century. Kipling added his own critique: "The moral dry rot of it all is having no law that need be obeyed: no line to toe: no trace to kick over and no compulsion to do anything."

He remarked that "a certain defect runs through everything—workmanship, roads, bridges, contracts, barter and sale and so forth—all inaccurate, all slovenly, all out of plumb and untrue." He said the natural wealth of the land made up for this ineptitude, "and the slovenly plenty hides their sins unless you look for them." To Kipling it was "barbarism plus telephone, electric light, rail and suffrage but all the more terrible for that reason. I like it."

Those descriptions of America might have been applied to his brother-in-law, Beatty Balestier. For all that the fun-loving Beatty was slovenly and perhaps a

In 1893, Kipling, center, was photographed surreptitiously by a young man concealed in a peanut stand on Main Street in Brattleboro; Kipling had come by sled for supplies and mail with his friend and neighbor, John Bliss.

barbarian at times, Rudyard liked him, too. And Kipling liked Vermont, telling Henley about the excitement when his team of carriage horses, Rod and Rick, suddenly sank to their ears in a snowdrift.

Still, he felt an uneasiness with the United States, "a grasping and annexatory land, eternally stirring up Canada to revolt and it will bear a lot of watching."

During the winter, Kipling finished reading the final page proofs of a new collection of short stories entitled *Many Inventions,* to be published that year. There was nothing in the new book from his months in Vermont, but work was flowing freely at Bliss Cottage, especially the Mowgli stories. He gave the original manuscript of the tale "Mowgli's Brothers" to Josephine's nurse, Miss Susan Bishop, in gratitude for her care of Carrie and the baby. He told Miss Bishop she could sell it if ever she needed cash. Years later, she did so.

Among the very few photographs taken of Kipling in Vermont without his permission was one surreptitiously snapped that winter outside the post office on Main Street. Kipling was standing by a sleigh, which was being loaded with supplies. According to John Bliss, the photo was taken by a young man concealed inside a peanut stand. It showed Rudyard bundled in a long fur coat and fur hat.

In late March, he finished the final draft for a book of collected poems to be published in 1896, entitled *The Seven Seas*. Most of these had been worked up or published elsewhere before the Kiplings settled in Vermont. Among these were "Song of the Cities" and "Song of the English" and "The Last Chantey."

The sea and ships were increasingly themes in Kipling's work, and among the verses finished at Bliss Cottage that winter was "The Anchor Song," about a sailing ship leaving harbor for the open sea. From the dust-caked, oppressed lives of British soldiers in the Indian Army, he was turning to sailors. Working now on a long poem, "McAndrew's Hymn," his narrator was a seasoned Scottish ship's engineer, who sees the divine hand in his vessel's great steam-powered engines, life in its machinery.

> *Lord, Thou hast made this world below the shadow of a dream,*
> *An', taught by time, I tak' it so—exceptin' always Steam.*
> *From coupler-flange to spindle-guide I see Thy Hand, O God—*
> *Predestination in the stride o' yon connectin'-rod.*

Far from the sea, in the snowbound hills of Vermont, Kipling's own shadows of dreams were drifting back to those long ocean voyages he had taken, and to thoughts of the British fleet that was the guardian of the far-flung empire. Times were changing, Germany was building her own fleet in challenge, and the United States showed no desire to be a British ally. To Kipling, there was more than ever a need for the powerful British navy, and he began to honor seamen as he had honored soldiers on the Afghan frontier.

Memories of India, visions and tales of wild jungle animals and tame beasts of burden also filled his working hours at Bliss Cottage. Outside, reveling in the cold and snow, he was moved by the breathtaking beauty of Vermont, but he was not yet inspired to set stories or verses here.

With the coming of spring, Kipling's time to write was limited, for there was a new house to build.

Beatty had prepared well for framing this house of the Kiplings' own design. He hired a ten-man crew of French-Canadian carpenters, who came down to erect the house on the new foundation. Led by a fellow named Jean Pigeon, the Quebecers amazed Kipling by putting up their own living structure "in what seemed twenty minutes."

Naulakha took shape swiftly, and Rudyard was usually on hand, excited and interested. As the long driveway was laid and stone outcrops were dynamited to level it, he and the crew "dived like woodchucks, into the deepest hole" when the charges were fired.

Then there was the region's first artesian well to be driven just south of the house for the water supply. "We sunk a five-inch shaft . . . into the New England granite, which nowhere was less than three, though some say thirty, thousand foot thick." At first, water was not plentiful. Farmers came to look and shake their heads in wonder at the project, and local papers regularly reported the progress of the drilling and how much water was produced per minute.

Folk thereabouts were taking interest in the Englishman who apparently took such little interest in them. The house was becoming a large one, and this surprised the locals, for it was obviously expensive. Had not the Kiplings settled here after losing all their money?

The Vermonters did not yet guess the Kiplings would, in eighteen months, become one of the wealthiest families in the region. That spring of 1893, Kipling wrote to his relations in England about the construction of Naulakha: "I'm in the thick of house building which is an invention of the Devil for the destruction of time and temper but things are shaping themselves slowly."

For all that he was consumed with the many details of Naulakha, Rudyard was well protected by Carrie, who saw to it he was seldom disturbed during the morning writing hours. *The Jungle Books* stories progressed steadily, and one by one they and their accompanying verses were finished and sent off to Mary Mapes Dodge for publication in *St. Nicholas*. He wrote "Tiger-Tiger," referring to it in a letter to Mrs. Dodge as the continuation of "Mowgli's Brothers," saying that the last in the "beast-tales" series "should follow in a little time."

He told the editor: "I've put into them pretty nearly everything that I know or have heard or dreamed about the Indian jungle."

The next would not, however, be the final story in *The Jungle Books*.

In his own nearby wilderness, Kipling took long walks with Carrie "when the first blood-root came up between patches of April snow, while yet the big drift at the bottom of the meadow held fast. In the shadow of the woods and under the blown pine needles, clots of snow lay till far into May, but neither the season nor the flowers took any note of them. . . ."

Those red wood-anemones pushing through the old snow in springtime became a favorite sight of Rudyard's, much as fields of goldenrod in late summer gave so much pleasure to Carrie.

Ever since boyhood in the Devon countryside, Kipling had taken keen interest in plants and creatures around him. He enjoyed bird-watching and wanted to learn to identify the local wildflowers and trees. He appreciated the coming of warmer weather:

". . . and, before we were well sure Winter had gone, the lackeys of my Lord Baltimore in their new liveries came to tell us that Summer was in the valley, and please might they nest in the bottom of the garden?"

Rudyard bought the guide *How to Know Wildflowers,* by Frances Theodora Dana. In a letter written to her from the Dunmore Hotel, where the Kiplings stayed while on an April visit to Manhattan, Rudyard complimented Mrs. Dana: "Will you permit a stranger to thank you very sincerely for the pleasure he has received from your book. . . ."

Last summer, he had tramped around without her guide, wondering about the flowers he saw. "The country-folk called them vaguely 'weeds' or cheerfully misnamed them." He also offered suggestions for the book, saying there should be an explanation of how to keep and press flower specimens. His suggestions, however, were not incorporated in future editions.

As Naulakha rose on its fieldstone foundation set on bedrock, Rudyard planned a rose garden next to his future study. There were eleven more acres available for planting and landscaping, and he and Carrie looked forward to it.

Rudyard also looked forward to the arrival of his father, John Lockwood Kipling, late that spring. His parents were returning to England from India now that his father had retired after almost thirty years in colonial service. Rudyard's mother, Alice, was to stay in England and establish a new home, while Lockwood continued on to Vermont to see their American grandchild.

"The Pater," as Rudyard called him, was a wise and kindly man who got along well with Carrie, though when he had first met her in England, he had described her to Alice as "a good man spoiled." At first, Kipling's mother did not take a liking to Carrie. Many months before the couple made their courtship public, Alice warned her husband, "That woman is going to marry our Ruddy," and she was not very happy about it.

Indeed, Carrie Balestier Kipling was not the idealized Victorian lady, expected to be delicate and coyly retiring in the presence of men. Capable in matters of business, Carrie had a fine mind and ready wit, but she was often stressed, as Henry James had noted, by a need for control. She sometimes exhibited possessiveness, and her moods could be unpredictable. Yet, as she proved at the death of her beloved Wolcott, she was rock-solid in crisis, almost to the exclusion of others who might help ease her pain.

From the start, Rudyard's easygoing patience balanced Carrie's nervousness. He was utterly loyal to her, being a man who gravitated toward strong women, and as complementary personalities, Rudyard and Carrie fit together. Not so with Carrie and younger brother Beatty.

Though Beatty at times could be an able construction manager, he was too often bolstered by hard cider, and that troubled Carrie. He should have been doing well financially because of the house project, but was as extravagant a spendthrift as ever, and she chastised him more than once for it. Carrie had him come to her several times a week for cash to pay the Naulakha accounts or himself. Sometimes the sums were only a few dollars. Paying him in bits and pieces rather than in a large periodic sum kept Beatty in rein and helped assure that he did not spend it on something for which it was not intended.

Carrie was treating her brother like a boy, and Beatty was often surly and resentful, especially when under the influence of alcohol, but he was apologetic and cheerful afterwards. Rudyard's impression that Americans too often had a volatile character to go with sometimes-shoddy workmanship no doubt came in part from frustrating dealings with Beatty.

Yet, Rudyard wanted to let family squabbles slide, and so did Beatty. After arguments between Carrie and Beatty, Rudyard and he made up man-to-man in cheerful laissez-faire. Then they went about the larger business of overseeing the work on the house. It was Carrie, however, who had the burden of keeping the books, who knew Beatty was not always prompt in paying off the accounts with the money she gave him. Sometimes, he did not pay them off at all.

As the construction progressed, Beatty's personal finances remained in disarray, and more than once he turned discreetly to Rudyard for a small loan or advance to take care of pressing bills. He would quietly approach the Kipling cottage and whistle at Rudyard's window to get him to come out without Carrie seeing them. Then he would ask for cash to take care of an immediate debt. On one occasion, Rudyard saw the sheriff waiting nearby for Beatty to get the money, and this horrified Carrie when she heard of it, as undoubtedly she heard about all of Beatty's troubles.

Still, Naulakha rose steadily, the finances shepherded by Carrie and the handiwork encouraged by Rudyard, who frequently pitched in.

Published in the *Boston Sunday Globe,* this silhouette of Kipling cleaning up debris near his new artesian well is from an unauthorized photograph taken by one of the well-drilling crew.

It was troubling that the new well still did not produce enough water. The drilling went on and on. Weeks passed, but little water was forthcoming. The drill bored ever deeper through solid rock. Some neighbors laughed, thinking Kipling was a money-wasting fool to keep on sinking that well, but he persisted.

A workman on the drilling crew violated a clearly stated taboo by secretly photographing Kipling through holes bored in the wall of the hut that stood over the machinery. The man sold the pictures to the *Boston Globe,* but it is said that Kipling found out and bought the negatives for a high price, then destroyed them. An artist at the *Globe* later made silhouette illustrations from the pictures, showing Kipling in sombrero and topcoat clearing away rubble from around the new well and also pushing a wheelbarrow.

This silhouette by a *Boston Sunday Globe* artist of Kipling at work on his Naulakha estate was drawn from an unauthorized photograph taken from concealment by a member of the well-drilling crew.

The French-Canadian craftsmen building the house were remarkably skillful, and remarkably inexpensive. Jean Pigeon talked over various woods with Kipling, saying the long attic could be finished in ash or cherry. Kipling was not familiar with either wood, but chose ash, which he later regretted when he came to see cherrywood in common use.

"Ignorant that I was . . . and so missed a stretch of perhaps the most satisfying interior wood that is grown." And this from a man who had seen the beautiful teaks and jungle woods used in India and Japan.

Years later, while making a speech in Canada, he fondly recalled Jean Pigeon, who said, "Everyt'ing which ze tree have experience' in ze forest 'e take wiz 'im into ze 'ouse."

In springtime, Kipling was fond of long walks, discovering the countryside and meeting strangers on the road—gypsies camped down by the Connecticut River, tinkers and quack peddlers in painted wagons.

"There are many such rovers, gelders of colts and the like, who work a long beat, south to Virginia almost, and north to the frontier, paying with talk and gossip for their entertainment."

It troubled him that sport hunters killed so much that they silenced the forest. A neighbor shot an eagle, five foot from wing tip to wing tip, and Rudyard was sorry about it. "I suppose he was concerned about his chickens," he later wrote, adding that all his neighbor "knew about the bird was just 'eagle.' "

"They seem to kill, for one reason or another, everything that moves in this land. Hawks, of course; eagles for their rarity; foxes for their pelts; red-shouldered blackbirds and Baltimore orioles because they are pretty, and the other small things for sport—"

As the house took form at the top of the sloping field, hikers stopped to look, and parties of full-time residents and tourists drove carriages or rode horses up the lane to see it. Kipling resented their nosiness, but in fact his scenic road had been for decades a favorite of day-trippers from the Brattleboro spas.

It was said the region had a different, beautiful seven- or ten-mile ride for every day of the summer holidays, and the fine view from the Bliss farm road was well known. By now, of course, there was no more fascinating sight thereabouts than the hideaway of the illustrious Rudyard Kipling.

As the creeper that girdles the tree trunk the Law runneth forward
  and back—
For the strength of the Pack is the Wolf, and the strength of the Wolf is
  the Pack.

Mowgli's Brothers, 1893

Chapter 8

The Pater and Naulakha

Lockwood Kipling arrived in New York City on June 18, 1893, and his coming was a joy for Rudyard, who had not seen him since December, 1891, in India. The tweedy Lockwood Kipling soon became a familiar figure on the roads and byways of Brattleboro and Dummerston, the Englishman stumping along with walking stick and pipe.

Kipling's neighbor, John Bliss, recalled Lockwood's visit, saying, "At first I could hardly understand his father, but I soon became used to his way of talking and grew to like him very much. He was a gentleman in every way."

Lockwood especially doted on little Josephine.

These days Rudyard wrote letters that were full of the baby's doings and cooings. "Jo," who was beginning to crawl, was taken out driving with her mother twice a day "for milk and eggs, or any other excuse—long drives of eight or ten miles when she sleeps and puts on a beautiful tan color."

One of their particular enjoyments was to go with Beatty's family and stay a few days in a boarding house at Lake Raponda, in the hills west of Dummerston. There, Rudyard took great interest in lumbermen, asking one to show how they rode on logs. This was a blessed time for Rudyard, with his father there to see him build both a family and a happy home.

Immediately, Lockwood was drawn to the new Mowgli stories, and was an inspiration and guide, especially with developing the concept in his son's poem "Law of the Jungle."

> *The Jackal may follow the Tiger, but, Cub, when thy whiskers are grown,*
> *Remember the Wolf is a hunter—go forth and get food of thine own.*
> *Keep peace with the Lords of the Jungle—the Tiger, the Panther, the Bear;*
> *And trouble not Hathi the Silent, and mock not the Boar in his lair.*
> * * *
> *Now these are the Laws of the Jungle, and many and mighty are they;*
> *But the head and the hoof of the Law and the haunch and the hump is—*
> * Obey!*

Rudyard's father John Lockwood Kipling, a valued critic and counsel, was himself a talented artist and able writer.

Illustration from *The Jungle Books.*

Interpretations of the "Law of the Jungle" and what it meant to Kipling have proliferated for a century. Was he demanding obedience to a government, to a culture, to a race, or to some primal power that governs life? Whatever Kipling's deeper meaning for the term "Law of the Jungle"—if there is a deeper meaning outside his fictional realm of anthropomorphic jungle creatures and Mowgli—this expression he coined has endured.

During his visit, Lockwood Kipling contributed something else to Naulakha. He placed an inscription in lime across the brick face of the fireplace in Rudyard's study. It was an excerpt from the Gospel of St. John: "The Night Cometh When No Man Can Work."

Perhaps this was a warning to Rudyard to create while he could, before unforeseen circumstances or the public taste went against him. Whatever Lockwood intended with the phrase, whenever Rudyard entered his Naulakha study it confronted him.

On his first trip ever to America, Lockwood thoroughly enjoyed himself, sometimes visiting Boston and New York with Rudyard. In Cambridge, Massachusetts, lived Harvard professor and philosopher Charles Eliot Norton, an old friend of Lockwood's. They had met years earlier when Norton was in India on business and again in England, where he had lived for a while with his family. Norton had counted among his friends some of the greatest thinkers and writers of the day, including Emerson and Longfellow.

As a child in England, Rudyard had played with Norton's daughter, Sallie, and now they renewed their friendship. It meant much to Kipling to have this close relationship between his family and the Nortons, for it served as a foundation of his life in Vermont.

Norton much admired Kipling's work, especially his recent realistic poetry and prose about steamships and the unsung men who operated them. (Carrington,

Kipling's Naulakha study, with the fireplace and its inscription, "The Night Cometh When No Man Can Work," placed there by his father, sculptor Lockwood Kipling.

Kipling's biographer, said this kind of writing was so new that it left the literary critics gasping.) Norton wrote: "What an interesting illustration Kipling affords of the poetic imagination working under difficulties!" He "has done a better work for his time than any other man in treating, through the poetic imagination, the material conditions which surround us all."

Thus did Kipling enter socially into the circles of the eastern intellectual establishment, where his opinions were stimulating and original, his latest published work avidly discussed. His friends included Harvard's William James, the author Sarah Orne Jewett, and a number of important diplomats, such as John Hay, whom he had first met on the ship from England to New York in 1892.

That summer, just before the house was ready, Kipling's restless father had them both go away for a tour, taking a trip north to Montreal, Quebec, and the Saguenay. They did some fishing, and it was a delight for them to be together on this American adventure. Carrie was left to make the move into the new house.

The architect's rendering of Naulakha.

She capably did so on August 12th, but on that very day the cook and serving girl suddenly quit, objecting to Carrie's insistence they now wear formal caps that were more appropriate for the grand new life at Naulakha.

After so much work designing and building, Naulakha was a dream come true.

The Kiplings wrote many invitations for friends and family to come and visit. Their neighbor and friend Molly Cabot heard Rudyard express thoughts of persuading his relations to settle here, at least seasonally, in a sort of cultural colony. In a letter to an English cousin, Rudyard said giddily, "Sweet lady—ho! ho! You mustn't expect me to be rational just now because we've but a week since moved into our new house and it is as a toy and a delight."

It was a relief to leave the cramped quarters of the rented cottage: "You can't imagine the bliss of getting into a place where you can turn round, unless you've spent a twelvemonth in a shanty one atop of the other. And unless you have lived with the laborious and futile foot bath in your room for that time you can't realize the bliss of a decent, clean porcelain tub and hot and cold water in the taps. It sounds absurd but when I luxuriously parboiled myself in a hot bath knowing I was beholden to no man therefore and shouldn't be charged for it on any bill I felt I was well paid for all my work and waitings."

Rudyard had designed their bathroom himself, for the first time in his life having the kind he had idealized. Soaking in the claw-foot tub was exquisite, though the well was still not producing enough water, and the boring went on. (Local papers were reporting the well's increasing depth—August 11, 140 feet; August 15, 180 feet—and these reports were hungrily picked up by newspapers from Boston to Philadelphia, for they grabbed any snatch of news about the elusive celebrity.)

Other than the inadequate yet ever-deepening well, the house was just the way Rudyard and Carrie wanted it.

"Then there is the delight of real doors that shut and cupboards where you want 'em; and built in bookcases and the like that make us very happy. So far we have found no mistake in our new dwelling and that is good because we made it for ourselves."

Years later, Kipling described the house in his autobiography, though slightly inaccurately: "Ninety feet was the length of it, thirty the width, on a high foundation of solid mortared rocks which gave us an airy and skunk-proof basement. The rest was wood, shingled roof and sides, with dull green hand-split shingles, and the windows were lavish and wide."

Actually Naulakha was less than twenty-five feet wide. It was sunny and cheerful on its foundation made of rocks from old fences, described by Kipling in a letter as "grey stone with moss on it that you can't distinguish from the lichened rocks of the pasture behind." All the rooms on both floors faced the east, with the spectacular panorama toward Mount Monadnock.

To Kipling, the "joy of the house" was the first floor's central loggia, a sort of inverted porch, with a ten-foot-wide window "that slides up bodily and lets all the woods and mountains in upon you in a flood." This sliding window disappeared neatly into a pocket in the wall above it. The Kiplings could sit in the loggia and enjoy the eastern view, the fresh breeze, and the sunshine without being seen by curious passersby on the road or by hunters crossing the field.

Designed elegantly but simply, Naulakha had wood paneling throughout, except in the loggia, which had on its walls the same green shingles as covered the outside. Naulakha's shingles were painted green to camouflage the house against the trees on the slope behind, making it less visible from the valley below. This clean-lined "Shingle Style" architectural design was an open and airy alternative to the ornate tastes of the high-Victorian era.

On Naulakha's first floor, a hall ran the length of the western side—the front. The main entrance was at the center, through a small porte cochere. The kitchen was at the north end, then came a dining room with brick fireplace, next the log-

A view of Naulakha from the south end, showing the porch and walled garden in front of Kipling's study on the first floor; the children's nursery is directly upstairs.

gia and an adjoining hall, and next Carrie's room, with a fireplace. Lastly, at the south end, was Rudyard's study, also with a fireplace.

Kipling told his friend, the local Congregational minister Charles O. Day, that the long, narrow house was like a ship riding on the hillside as if on a cresting wave. At the stern was the vessel's power plant—the kitchen and hot-air furnace—and at the prow was his study. Many a reporter hungered to get into that house, but only the closest of friends were allowed there, some chosen few even permitted to sit in the study while Kipling wrote at the oak desk by a window looking into the fieldstone-walled garden.

In the study, a bay window faced the eastward view; the top halves of the two windows on the west side were fitted with Tiffany stained glass, the lower halves covered by built-in bookshelves that filled the room's western wall. No one could see in from that side, thus affording Kipling more privacy to work. A small

Kipling in his study at Naulakha in 1895.

revolving bookcase was near the bay window, and a pair of easy chairs stood at the hearth. Rising from his desk, Kipling could pass from his study onto a piazza and then into the walled garden, where he took interest in planting beds of roses separated by paths. In time, there would be a longer walkway from the garden toward a gazebo of fieldstone among the trees. There was yet much to do, and the landscaping and planting of shrubs and trees on the bare slope became one of Kipling's greatest pleasures. He planted most things himself.

Since his youth, Kipling was almost mystically attracted to rising before dawn and sitting quietly, alone, to meditate. Early in life, he learned "my fortunate hour would be on the turn of sunrise, with a sou'-west breeze afoot."

The balmy weather usually comes to Brattleboro from the south, and Kipling's study and piazza were oriented that way. This was a perfect place to think on Mowgli and India, intuitively letting his muse, or daemon, guide thoughts and composition.

The coming night when no man could work, about which Lockwood's inscription on the fireplace warned, was not yet upon the dynamic Rudyard Kipling. In response to this phrase, much of his writing from Naulakha was eventually collected in a volume entitled *The Day's Work*.

After his father left for England that November, Rudyard told Carrie he had received a tremendous surge of renewed power. She wrote in her diary that Rudyard now experienced the "return of a feeling of great strength such as he had when he first came to London and met the men he was pitted against."

Unlike 1889, however, this reservoir of creative ability came from profound happiness rather than from fierce ambition. Kipling was more content than ever he had been, and the new home and the baby at the center of his life had much to do with it. Carrie wrote of Rudyard "humming and strumming" his verse all through the house. He was still busy with *The Jungle Books* and now with a second set of *Barrack-room Ballads*.

Some of Rudyard's verse written in Vermont was beginning to be published to enthusiastic reviews. "McAndrew's Hymn," about the ship's engineer and his vessel's mighty engine, was sold to *Scribners* for $500, the most ever paid for a poem in the United States.

In her room adjacent to Rudyard's study, Carrie efficiently kept the account books, wrote personal and business letters, and worked at needlepoint or knitted. While Rudyard wrote in the mornings, anyone who tried to get through Carrie's

Carrie Kipling sits at her writing desk in her Naulakha office, where she prevented unwanted visitors from interrupting her husband when he was writing in the next room.

room was seldom allowed to disturb him. The Kiplings joked that her room was called "The Dragon's Chamber" by unwanted visitors.

Carrie did all she could to keep the household quiet during Rudyard's writing hours. With work still going on to finish the last construction and drill the well, and with an infant in the house, it was not easy.

Upstairs, above Rudyard's study, the baby's bedroom and day nursery opened onto a verandah, also facing south. Next on that floor, moving northward in the house, was a spacious bedroom for the Kiplings, along with their wainscotted well-appointed bathroom. Then came a guest bedroom, and two bedrooms for live-in servants.

On the third floor was a smaller room and the long open attic covered with Jean Pigeon's ash boards. The attic was lit by five dormer windows. There, Kipling had his billiards table, a favorite pastime he also enjoyed when at the Brooks House in Brattleboro.

Rudyard gave permission for an architect's sketch of the exterior to be published accompanying an article in a periodical called *The Critic,* which credited the Catalogue Committee of the Architectural League of New York for furnishing the rendering of Naulakha. Kipling did not, however, permit anything of the interior floor plan to be publicized.

"People make a great mistake about Mr. Rudyard Kipling," *The Critic's* writer began. "He does not hate America. On the contrary, he likes the country; else why should he make his home here?"

The article said Kipling had his choice of anywhere in the world to live, but he preferred Vermont, "and in this selection he shows his appreciation of the beauties of nature." The article praised the charms of the Green Mountains, then being discovered by artists "and other lovers of beautiful scenery."

The writer estimated the cost of construction to be $10,000, adding that Naulakha would be Kipling's permanent home winter and summer, with him "descending into New York only when imperative business calls."

"At Brattleboro his child was born, and on the Brattleboro hillside will his household gods hold sway. Where the home is, there the heart is, also; so, far from being 'down on America,' Mr. Kipling has evinced his affection for the country in the most emphatic way."

Save for the misstatement that Naulakha is in Brattleboro (it is just over the line in Dummerston), *The Critic* caught the spirit of Rudyard's intent and apparent expectations for the rest of his life.

He even offered to purchase the Bliss Cottage from John Bliss, for the sentimental reason that Josephine, now sometimes called "Bips" or "Taffy," was born there. Bliss Cottage was not for sale.

Using the Hindi term "Naulakha" for his home gave Kipling much satisfaction—the satisfaction of East and West meeting here, and the satisfaction of honoring Wolcott's memory.

Beyond the collaboration with Wolcott on their novel, the name Naulakha had rich and fond associations for Rudyard. In 1887, he had visited another Naulakha, this one in India. It was a massive tower at the entrance to the ruined citadel of Chitor Garh in Rajputana. Known as the Naulakha Bandhar, or treasure house, the riches of the rulers of Mewar once had been stored here.

There was another Naulakha known to Kipling: a district in the Indian city of Lahore had that name. As were most Anglo-Indians, Kipling was familiar with the city's ancient Naulakha Pavilion. This small marble structure, inlaid with precious stones in the form of flowers, was an attraction for tourists. On his final visit to Lahore, Kipling had lingered at the pavilion, chatting with some British soldiers.

These ancient Naulakhas had inspired Rudyard and Wolcott to give this name to a legendary jewel sought by the hero of their novel, *The Naulahka*. As a chapter heading, Kipling wrote verse about the quest for something elusive and precious:

> *Because I sought it far from men,*
> *In deserts and alone;*
> *I found it burning overhead,*
> *The jewel of a throne.*
>
> *Because I sought—I sought it so*
> *And spent my days to find—*
> *It blazed one moment ere it left*
> *The blacker night behind.*

A few Vermonters understood the name to be "Nellaker," and that it belonged to a princess of vanished local Indians.

From "Toomai of the Elephants" in *The Jungle Books.* Illustrator: W.H. Drake

Calm-eyed he scoffs at Sword and Crown,
  Or, panic-blinded stabs and slays;
Blatant he bids the world bow down,
  Or cringing begs a crust of praise;

Or sombre-drunk, at mine and mart,
  He dubs his dreary brethren Kings.
His hands are black with blood—his heart
  Leaps, as a babe's, at little things.

An American, 1893

Chapter 9

The Day's Work

Kipling was becoming a mature married man and father, with a dignified receding hairline to match.

In a letter that fall of 1893 to an Australian writer and friend whose own marriage was impending, he said: "I shouldn't be surprised if matrimony didn't do you a heap of good. Tisn't a panacea that I recommend right and left by any means but it teaches a man to keep his temper and to remember that the earth does not revolve absolutely and eternally round his hat. It teaches the tougher virtues— such as humility, restraint, order and forethought and like literature is its own exceeding great reward."

In a December letter to editor W. E. Henley, to whom he was sending the latest of the *Barrack-room Ballads*, "The Sergeant's Weddin'," he bubbled about Josephine and her "teeth, four of 'em," and how she was "crawling about my room now—a little ashputtle—prying into the wood basket and trying to get into the ashes and hauling down my books on her innocent head or stopping to sing runes in her own tongue."

On the Naulakha property just then a new stable was being built, the storm drains near it were frozen, "and we are waiting for a windmill to pump water out of a 325 foot artesian well which we have been boring. . . ."

A "female cow" was not calving on time, a sump pump was frozen, and their new gravel road had been wiped out by snow drifts. Despite the problems, the Kiplings rejoiced in their house "which we can pat and play with." Since they paid no rent, he added, they could afford to buy books, one of his favorite pastimes.

He told Henley he was "doing better than writing with my good right hand. . . . Chiefly—and this I would impress upon you—I am sitting still and keeping quiet, for the good of my soul."

Those who knew Kipling well might doubt that he could ever sit still for long or keep quiet, though in this time he was apparently reflecting deeply upon his work and throwing away much verse. (Writing verse, whether kept or discarded, always gave him much pleasure.)

"For our Social Engagements . . . we went out to dinner for the first time in three months last Sunday—eight miles there and as many back—a blazing moon on white snow and the road dipping in and out of the pine hollows where the frozen brooks were."

He was working manually, and enjoying it. "I've grubbed up a hundred and fifty yards of old stone wall with pick and spade; raked leaves off slopes; lopped undergrowth and burned refuse and planted pines as long as the weather served and it's mighty consoling to look along a straight line that you have cleaned by your own lone self as the children say here."

The Kiplings made plans to visit New York, where Carrie had family and there were many new friends in the publishing world. Rudyard was widely sought after as a celebrity guest. They would stay in the city "for a few weeks and there we join the Giddy Whirl and are no end fine and dissipated. They have an intensely Literary society there—same old names cropping up week after week at the same old parties; same old gags; same old dishwater as it might be in any city we could name—allowing for local color and the necessity of creating the Great American Literature."

In his usual exasperated way, Kipling urged Henley not to "spare the rod" in criticism of any American writing: "This 'ere is the land where 'everything goes' and the lawlessness leaks into the books as it does into all the other things. Only, there's no force at the back of the incessant posing to be free—only common people doing common things in the cheapest and most effective way for immediate results." Kipling talked just as harshly about whatever he disliked in the India colonial service, or about British military bureaucracy, or liberals in Parliament—and about anything he considered inadequate, such as "carelessness in administration, sloppiness of speech, vague appeals to the sentiments of great multitudes. . . ." Still, American friends and acquaintances cringed with annoyance when he abused their government or people—whether or not that criticism was to the point.

Kipling's objection to political humbug erupted in particularly eloquent assaults on anyone who declared "The People" to be omnipotent. "There's nothing in the 'People' and the talk about the 'People' a jot more to be reverenced than in Kings and the Divine Right of the same. They are only men anyway—not Gods above the law of wrong doing and, so it seems, much of the windy talk in England about the inherent rightness and righteousness of lots of folks in a lump is skittles—nothing more than the old bunkum about the Divine Right of Kings transferred to an ungetable fetish which isn't responsible for its own actions.

"You can't indict the People and cut off their heads for evil practices, and for myself I like a responsible person whose head I can help to cut off if need be."

For all that Kipling had a knack of raising the hackles of the self-righteous and self-serving, Molly Cabot said the publication of his next book was always widely anticipated with great excitement and talked about for weeks before it appeared. Confident, and in some matters very self-righteous, himself, Kipling was more irascible, more audacious than ever these days. His writing crackled with barbed wit and rough language.

In Kipling's new set of soldier verses for the next *Barrack-room Ballads*, none was rougher than "The Sergeant's Weddin'," in which enlisted men who hate their rogue of a sergeant savor the thought of his marriage to a whore of a bride, considering it just retribution for him.

> 'E was warned agin 'er—
> That's what made 'im look;
> She was warned agin' 'im—
> That is why she took.
> Wouldn't 'ear no reason,
> Went an' done it blind;
> We know all about 'em,
> They've got all to find.
>
> Cheer for the Sergeant's weddin'—
> Give 'em one cheer more!
> Grey gun-'orses in the lando,
> An' a rogue is married to, etc.

This sort of vulgarity already had turned some refined folk against Kipling. He did not care. His daemon inspired him, and follow it he must, lest he risk losing the intuitive gift that guided him. Kipling wrote what he wrote because he enjoyed it, and because he believed in it.

That winter of 1893–94, the Kiplings erected a steel windmill to pump water from their well, now 350 feet deep and producing adequately at last. The task of raising the windmill just at the onset of cold weather was a bitterly hard one. By now, life in the Vermont countryside was not as idyllic for Kipling the home-builder as it had been for Kipling the dreamy newcomer in a rented cottage.

Rudyard wrote to a friend about erecting the windmill: ". . . every minute and thought has been taken up in fighting the weather, which has suddenly gone mad—because I suppose it saw us trying to put up a windmill. Figure to yourself (eight or nine men trying to work in despite of it all) blinding wind and cold;

followed by a heavy snow; then a day and a night and a day of 25 below zero, then an ice storm and then drenching rain and thaw and freeze coating everything half an inch deep. Oh, but I am almost out of patience. Yesterday I spent hauling on a rope to hoist an idiotic three legged thing like this [sketch of windmill on its side]. It looks awfully drunk still and a man is spending this Sabbath puttering over its nuts and screws. Don't you never go for to dig a well and make towers and windmills." The windmill went up eventually, but then it creaked and creaked and creaked as it turned, and was not a pleasant sound on that tranquil Naulakha hillside.

Winter was not all struggle, though, for Kipling was increasingly adept with snowshoes and loved following paths through the woods. Rudyard and Carrie especially enjoyed family drives in their basket sleigh on the six-mile circuit to Crosby Pond and back. Sometimes, Rudyard liked to drive over the Connecticut River at Brattleboro, traveling up the side of Wantastiquet, "our guardian mountain across the river." From there, he enjoyed the panorama looking back at Naulakha as it rode the cresting wave of a hillside.

In his autobiography, he recalled one of these outings, when the road brought them to a farmhouse, "where we were welcomed by the usual wild-eyed, flat-fronted woman of the place."

Convinced these backwoods women were all half-mad with loneliness, Kipling described her as speaking "fiercely" when she asked, "Be you the new lights 'crost the valley yonder? Ye don't know what a comfort they've been to me this winter. Ye aren't ever goin' to shroud 'em up—or *be* ye?"

Kipling made sure that for as long as they lived at Naulakha, the side "that looked her-ward was always nakedly lit."

In spite of their desire for privacy, Rudyard and Carrie could appear quite ostentatious when visiting town in winter. Not only did they both wear plush, costly fur coats and hats, but they acquired a tiger rug, which they laid in full sight in their smart basket sleigh. They even hired an English groom named Robins to drive them. Rudyard was a poor hand at driving either sleigh or buggy—Molly Cabot had to help him one day when he got stuck across the road while trying to turn. Although Carrie was good at it, she preferred to go to town in high style, driven by Robins. Some said she put on the airs of English gentry much more than her husband did. The spectacular Kipling tiger skin startled Vermonters, who at last realized they were wealthy. Indeed, in the twelve months through November, Rudyard had earned more than $3,000.

Though little involved in social affairs, the Kiplings enjoyed doing good deeds and sharing good cheer. They gave a Christmas party for the children of the

Brattleboro village school, which Kipling liked visiting. Once, they invited the Episcopal church choirboys to Naulakha. The house windows were hung with evergreen branches, there was a decorated Christmas tree, and everyone sang carols by candlelight. The boys watched Rudyard playing on the floor with year-old Josephine, and decades later, one of them recalled being amazed that Mr. Kipling looked so very young to be so famous.

Rudyard wrote a comment in Carrie's last diary entry at the close of 1893: "Another perfect year ended. The Lord has been very good to us. Amen. R.K."

Relations were warm with Madam Balestier, the grandmother in Beechwood, and also with Carrie's mother, Anna, and sister, Josephine, both of whom visited regularly from their home in New York.

For a number of reasons, however, matters were increasingly shaky with Beatty and Mai. When sober, Beatty could be capable at managing the Kipling projects, but he was not sober enough for Carrie's liking. He had less work to do for the Kiplings now that the house was almost complete, and that meant less income for him. Beatty had not always been conscientious. (Kipling later said he "worked beautifully for the first six weeks" of a major project, "and then he tailed off and did not do much.") Yet they wanted him to benefit from what work was still to be done: a carriage house with horse stalls had to be finished, and they decided to build a tennis court.

Beatty could count on small amounts of cash from the Kiplings for various responsibilities—for example, he earned a bonus of fifty cents per workman hired for them. He was always short of cash, however, and Madam Balestier helped him with loans. Eventually, Carrie and her grandmother both countersigned for him as guarantors of a bank mortgage on Maplewood, his farm.

The Kiplings made some cash advances to Beatty, and he worked them off, which was acceptable. After all, one reason they had come here to begin with was to help him get on his feet financially. Too often, however, they were unhappy, for whenever he fizzled out it took much too long to finish a job. Mainly, drink was the reason for Beatty's slackness.

Though he was proud of his ability to hold liquor, Beatty could be unpleasant when hung over. Kipling later described him as often being "just plain ugly in the morning, like a man who has got more in him than he ought to have."

When drunk, Beatty sometimes hovered on the edge of violence, and that also worried the Kiplings. One day, when driving his buggy home in a drunken stupor, Beatty could not get the door of his barn open. Anger and frustration mounted as he struggled with the door, until at last he madly tore off planks until the entire side of the barn was ripped completely open. Then he drove in.

Another point of friction was that little Marjorie Balestier was being brought up to run wild compared with Josephine, who was strictly disciplined and carefully protected by her parents and nurse. The Kiplings felt that Marjorie was a bad influence on Josephine. Naturally, Mai Balestier resented any advice from Carrie in the matter of Marjorie's upbringing, well intended or blatantly patronizing as that advice might be. Old feelings of hostility between Carrie and Beatty were being stirred up again.

In this time, Kipling wrote the poem "An American," with the opening line, "The American Spirit speaks:"

Once again, his choice of an American prototype might well have been his brother-in-law, Beatty, but the larger subject was the United States. Kipling thought the wealthy States were being overwhelmed by greedy (non-Anglo-Saxon) immigrants who did not share or comprehend the best Anglo-Saxon traditions, education, or culture.

Kipling's "American Spirit" says of the American:

> His easy unswept hearth he lends
> From Labrador to Guadeloupe
> Till, elbowed out by sloven friends,
> He camps, at sufferance, on the stoop.

Kipling did not like to see what he considered the open-handed, easygoing American being taken advantage of, and he shuddered at the frequent bloody labor strikes that skirted anarchy as the radical leaders, mostly foreign-born, called for the destruction of capitalism. "An American" might be read as a warning from Rudyard Kipling to his adopted homeland. The speaker, however, is not intended to be Kipling, but rather the true spirit of the people, an avatar or race god, who describes the American:

> But through the shift of mood and mood,
> Mine ancient humour saves him whole—
> The cynic devil in his blood
> That bids him mock his hurrying soul;
> That bids him flout the Law he makes,
> That bids him make the Law he flouts,
> Till, dazed by many doubts, he wakes
> The drumming guns that have no doubts;

Kipling warns the young United States against arrogantly stirring up international hostility that could result in war and make the country "the scandal of the elder earth." The American Spirit, as Kipling characterized it, offered hope for the nation, perhaps even hope for the likes of Beatty Balestier:

> *Enslaved, illogical, elate,*
> *He greets the embarrassed Gods, nor fears*
> *To shake the iron hand of Fate*
> *Or match with Destiny for beers.*
>
> *Lo, imperturbable he rules,*
> *Unkempt, disreputable, vast—*
> *And, in the teeth of all the schools,*
> *I—I shall save him at the last!*

That winter of 1893–94, Kipling wrote to Henry James in England, saying the undisciplined United States should be considered akin to a backward Asian country, "all huge promises and poor fulfilment wherein there is no time sense and no sense of responsibility."

He went on: "It makes me weep to think how all these years gone the sober conscientious western powers have been treating this last of the Asiatic kingdoms as a grown-up person. *We* work it from the Oriental standpoint, and it answers perfectly to that helm."

Kipling invited James to visit Naulakha and not be intimidated because there was a child in the house: "It is true we worship a baby in a snow temple but that service does not run continuously and the idol has her shrine into which she is shut while the worshippers eat and drink and write."

James never did come to Naulakha.

Far from the bustle of the cosmopolitan world he knew so well, Kipling's writing was proceeding successfully. He spoke to James about Vermont: "The land is like a cool grey studio to rest in and, thanks to its back of beyondity, one can chuck into waste paper baskets much that would otherwise and otherwhere come into print." He added: "We are no nearer America of the market place than we are to China up here."

In this appealing insulation from the outside world, Kipling found great enjoyment in the company of Dr. James Conland.

Their friendship was that of two broad-ranging minds that appreciated both rugged good humor and profound philosophical discussions. Kipling had much

Rudyard and Josephine on the porch outside his study.

in common with Conland, both of them virtually self-educated without frills, each learning about life the hard way, and learning well.

Conland was born in Brooklyn in 1851, of Irish parents, who died when he was only seven. He went to work on a farm in Cape Cod and later served on fishing vessels, coasters, and East India traders. Conland's youthful adventures had taken him close to bloody revolution in Cuba, and like Kipling he had seen first-hand the stark horrors of war. Conland's many stories of the sea were fascinating to Kipling, who gradually conceptualized a story around the dangerous life of a cod-fishing crew.

During the winters, when the boats were in dry dock, young Conland had taught himself at country schools. In 1875 he came to Brattleboro, working as a

Dr. James Conland was Kipling's best friend in New England and, as a former cod fisherman, helped with research for *Captains Courageous,* a novel about the Massachusetts cod-fishing fleet.

clerk in the Willard Drug Store, and mastering pharmacology. He was an omnivorous reader—much like Kipling—and rapidly worked his way through the University of Vermont, graduating in 1878.

Upon his return to Brattleboro, Conland practiced medicine with a local doctor, becoming a partner. He was much esteemed by patients and neighbors, and was known as a common-sense physician who avoided prescribing harsh medicines if it was better for the body to recuperate on its own. His hooded sleigh was a familiar sight at the farms, as he faithfully visited sick patients, no matter how treacherous the roads or how severe the weather.

It was remarkable that in spite of his being a staunch Democrat in a land of Republicans, Conland was elected to the state legislature in 1884. There, according to the *Annals of Brattleboro* written years later by Molly Cabot, "Although he seldom spoke at any length, his opinions carried weight."

So Rudyard Kipling had a best friend in New England, but more than that, he had been hooked by an intriguing sea story that would not let him go until it was written.

The King has called for priest and cup,
The King has taken spur and blade
To dub True Thomas a belted knight,
And all for the sake of the songs he made.

The Last Rhyme of True Thomas, 1894

Chapter 10

Homesick

Early in 1894, Kipling wrote the verses "Pan in Vermont," likening the itinerant seed salesman to Pan, the cloven-footed lord of the nature spirits, who casts a spell and holds out elusive dreams of bounty and harvest. The seed salesman appeared regularly with the thaw, selling small paper packages of flower and vegetable seed, and making large promises about their potential.

> *It's forty in the shade today, the spouting eaves declare;*
> *The boulders nose above the drift, the southern slopes are bare;*
> *Hub-deep in slush Apollo's car swings north along the Zodiac.*
> *Good lack, the Spring is back, and Pan is on the road!*
>
> * * *
>
> *Serene, assenting, unabashed, he writes our orders down:—*
> *Blue Asphodel on all our paths—a few true bays for crown—*
> *Uncankered bud, immortal flower, and leaves that never fall—*
> *Apples of Gold, of Youth, or Health—and—thank you, Pan—that's all.*
>
> *He's off the drifted track to catch the Windsor train,*
> *And swindle every citizen from Keene to Lake Champlain;*
> *But where his goat's-hoof cut the crust—beloved, look below—*
> *He's left us (I'll forgive him all) the may-flower 'neath her snow!*

The piping, conjuring Pan of a seed salesman charmed folk with his ideas and dreams and, in a different way, so did Rudyard Kipling's harper in the poem "The Last Rhyme of True Thomas." Unlike the salesman, Thomas played upon a harp that would not lie.

In this poem Kipling expresses his unwillingness to accept official honors or be identified with any political party or become the British poet laureate, a post as yet unfilled since the death of Tennyson. "The Last Rhyme of True Thomas" is a ballad about a medieval poet who declines the royal offer of knighthood.

True Thomas, powerful harper of magic in the Land of Fairie, will never play or compose for the sake of political glory—especially when he has the superior power that gives him enchantment over the very king himself. Thomas plays upon his magic harp until at last the proud king is overwhelmed, dismayed, and humbled by its song of truth. Thomas says,

> *"I ha' harpit ye up to the Throne o' God,*
> *"I ha' harpit your midmost soul in three;*
> *"I ha' harpit ye down to the Hinges o' Hell,*
> *"And—ye—would—make—a—Knight o' me!"*

In late February, the Kiplings left Naulakha and Josephine, with her nurse, under Beatty's charge and went for a holiday to Bermuda. Rudyard had expressed particular interest in seeing the British forts there.

Soon after they set off, the windmill blew down and had to be laboriously raised once again.

In Bermuda for three weeks, the Kiplings began an acquaintance with the Catlins, a Morristown, New Jersey, family that remained lifelong friends. Also, Rudyard was grateful to spend hours with English soldiers in the island's garrison. He and Carrie were invited to dinner with them, and it was like old times in India as he sat and talked and questioned and enjoyed their company.

Many of the garrison's veterans had served in India, though their memories of border warfare were gloomy ones. The regiment was the Royal Berkshires, and from them Kipling learned the terrible story of their heroic last stand during a rout in the Afghan frontier wars fourteen years earlier. To Kipling, then, came the haunting verses of "That Day," which some soldiers called his greatest ever about fighting men.

In the voice of a common soldier he tells the story of the disaster, with grim memories of defeat and flight from the battlefield:

> *Now there ain't no chorus 'ere to give,*
> *Nor there ain't no band to play;*
> *An' I wish I was dead 'fore I done what I did,*
> *Or seen what I seed that day!*

The Kiplings went back to Naulakha in early April, refreshed and rested and ready for a summer sojourn in England. But when they got to Vermont and found Beatty had run the household into unnecessary debt, they were extremely annoyed with him. After settling the accounts, Rudyard and Carrie sailed with Josephine and her nurse to England.

At sea, Kipling was leaning on the rail when "our steamer came almost atop of a whale, who submerged just in time to clear us, and looked up into my face with an unforgettable little eye. . . ." A few years later, while making sketches to illustrate the *Just So Stories,* he "remembered and strove after that eye." It appears in pen and ink drawings with the story "How the Whale Got Its Throat."

In a letter from England to May Catlin, one of three daughters of the Morristown family, Kipling's first words were, "I do not like London," and he could not stand "the greyness of the air." They left the city to stay in a rented country house in Wiltshire, close to his parents, now living at Tisbury.

In Britain, Kipling found himself embraced and honored by both the highest of society and by the lowest man in the street. He was considered the empire's conscience, an eloquent and patriotic writer sensitive to the fleeting truth of the moment. This former reporter for an obscure Indian newspaper was invited to a formal dinner by lords and ladies as the guest of honor along with the great commander of troops, Lord Roberts.

At this dinner, Kipling and Roberts strode together into the banquet hall between two rows of standing guests, appearing, as Carrington said, "almost as equals." It was an astonishing leap in social stature for Rudyard, who was not yet thirty. He had to admit he enjoyed it, an attitude far different from that of his bohemian early days, when he disdained public praise.

During a cold, bleak English summer, Kipling worked as hard as ever, producing several poems, four new *Jungle Book* tales, and a broad farce "which made me laugh for three days." That farce, "My Sunday at Home," is the story of a well-meaning American doctor who, while visiting England, is swept up in a panic to try to save the life of an apparently delirious workman thought to have swallowed poison. Confusion and embarrassment result largely because of the American's forwardness, for the patient is actually drunk, not dying.

Another humorous story written in this time was "An Error in the Fourth Dimension," in which a wealthy American tries to settle down in England and become assimilated, as many were doing at that time. Like the doctor, he fails to grasp the protocols of English culture (the "fourth dimension") and as a result is so publicly embarrassed that he is forced to quit the country, leaving behind his handsome house and all. He returns to America, where he can be himself: a rich man wielding all the raw influence new money can buy.

While in England, Kipling was restless, unhappy with the chilly weather. On one unusually warm day he wrote to an American editor:

"—real warmth at last, and it waked in me a lively desire to be back in Main Street, Brattleboro', Vt., U.S.A., and hear the sody-water fizzing in the drug-store and discuss the outlook for the Episcopalian church with the clerk; and get a bottle of lager in the basement of the Brooks House, and hear the doctor tell fish-yarns and have the iron-headed old farmers loaf up and jerk out: 'Bin in Yurope haint yer?' and then go home, an easy gait, through the deep white dust with the locust trees just stinking to heaven, and the fireflies playing up and down the Swamp Road, and the Katy-dids giving oratorios, free gratis and for nothing, to the whippoorwill, and everybody sitting out in the verandah after dinner, smoking Durham tobacco in a cob pipe with our feet on the verandah railings, and the moon coming up behind Wantastiquet. There's one Britisher at least homesick for a section of your depraved old land, and he's going, Please Allah! the first week in August, by the Kaiser Wilhelm, and won't New York be hot—just! There's a smell of horse-piss, Italian fruit vendor, nickel cigars, sour lager and warm car-conductor drifting down Carmine Street at this minute from Sixth Avenue, which I can smell with the naked eye as I sit here. I shall go to Long Island, to a friend's and eat new corn, and I wish you were coming, too."

It was a joy to return to peaceful Naulakha, so distant from the almost-dizzying adulation and honors Rudyard experienced in England. On Main Street, he was by now looked upon as just another outsider living in a big new house on the back roads.

The Kiplings loved to watch two-and-a-half-year-old Josphine growing into such a beauty. Rudyard told her animal fables, which to her parents' delight she repeated so well the next day. Though Kipling at first did not write them down, these were the makings of the *Just So Stories*, told to little "Taffy," best-beloved daughter of "Tegumai," the storyteller. Josephine said her father's poems were of two kinds— "howly growly" ones, or "tinkley-tinkley-tinky."

Upon his return to Naulakha, Kipling first produced "A Walking Delegate," one of only two stories he set in America. It takes place in Beatty's meadow, where a "mob of horses" was always about. The horses are made to portray the characters of the American labor movement: agitators, radicals, and ordinary workers.

As much as Kipling had high hopes for future happiness living in Vermont, he continued to express sourness at aspects of American culture. Writing to a cousin

Pictured by an artist from *Vanity Fair* magazine during a 1894 visit to England, Kipling was enthusiastically and publicly honored as the most popular writer of his day.

Josephine Kipling in the loggia at Naulakha.

in England, he commented in a postscript that he had seen a production of Shakespeare's *Twelfth Night* in New York. He said with dismay, "Malvolio was done with a strong Irish accent. I left before the end of the play. An Irish accent."

Because of an ongoing drought that summer, Rudyard had some satisfaction in what he had built at Naulakha—unlike most neighbors his well was not dry.

"We are dusty and white with drouth. Ancient springs that never failed before have gone under and farmers are at their wits end to know how to water their stock.

"Behold the reward of forethought! They laughed at me when I drove my 300-ft. artesian. Now I laugh as I watch a lantern staggering across a meadow at midnight where a man goes to tickle up a moribund ram [pump] which is being choked with leaves and mud. My well is pure and icy cold and unfailing. Also I have the joy of looking down on my neighbors—which alone is worth the price of admission."

The steel windmill, which Rudyard called the "Unnecessary Pillywinkie," had been put out of commission since a hot-air engine had been installed to pump the water. He wanted to get rid of the windmill, and half-jokingly offered to send it to his friend Charles Eliot Norton, who was interested in having a windmill at his country house in Ashfield, Massachusetts.

It was "a kind and affectionate windmill" whose only problem is "in his present position he doesn't get enough wind to keep him busy. Now on your grey hills he would entirely lose his present laziness and become an extremely valuable servant."

Kipling said, "No one wants him here—least of all this household. We want to pull him over but even then he'd have to be buried, and he is nearly sixty feet high."

Before Norton had made up his mind, Kipling wrote "the Infamous Pillywinkie is (thank Heaven) dead." A gale "sprang up as he was being dismantled and the man who was bestraddling his vicious old head was all but slain by being whirled to death and guillotined at the same time."

Kipling and a work crew put a block and tackle on the Pillywinkie and "pulled him over bodily. It was a beautiful sight."

Soon after their return from England, the Kiplings advertised in New York for a new coachman. They hired another Englishman, Matthew Howard, formerly employed by a British lord. According to Carrington, Howard's "livery and style and indubitable cockney accent caused no little stir in Brattleboro."

A short man, the same size as Kipling, Howard was erect and proud, refusing to wear old clothes for dirty work. He wore "top boots and cord breeches even when cleaning out the stable," said Carrington. Hired with a wife and claiming to have no children, Howard lived in a cottage built for him halfway down the driveway. He was excellent with the three horses, and one day in October prevented disaster when the carriage team, Rod and Rick, bolted after Rick got a rear leg over the pole and panicked.

The horses ran, with Howard fighting them back. Aboard were Carrie, Josephine, and the baby's nurse. The women coolly wrapped up Josephine and laid her on the floor of the jarring, rocking carriage, then sat in silence, holding on, as the horses stampeded madly for a mile. Howard kept them under tight rein, until at last a rear wheel collapsed, spilling everyone out. Thanks to his skill and courage, no one was hurt beyond some stiffness and bruises that ached for a week or so. Howard was embarrassed and angry with himself at the incident, but his ability under pressure won him the admiration of the Kiplings. As time passed, when they needed a serving girl or a maid, it was he who conveniently found an English one, and then another. They were, in fact, his daughters. Eventually, the Kiplings discovered there were six Howard children, and one by one they were brought over from England. The family became indispensable to the Kiplings and Naulakha.

As for Beatty, the emergence of Matthew Howard left even less for him to do, and the two of them did not get along. Carrington said, "Everyone liked Howard, except Beatty, and Howard was the one person at 'Naulakha' who was never impressed with Beatty's blarney."

There were times when they argued and nearly came to blows.

To some extent it could be said that building the house was a collaboration with Beatty Balestier, as writing the novel had been a collaboration with Wolcott. But, for the Kiplings, their often-frustrating labors with Beatty did not lend the name "Naulakha" any additional fond meaning.

Beatty became increasingly distressing, especially to Carrie. He often drank before coming to meet with her on business, further irritating her. She was already troubled by the nagging questions about his use of the money she gave to pay their building accounts. It was doubtful that Beatty was faithfully disbursing all the money to suppliers in a timely manner.

When asked about this directly, he was cheerfully evasive and vague about financial matters. He kept few clear written records or receipts, saying it was unnecessary, because much was arranged by word-of-mouth, and besides, he was family, not just some hired general contractor. Kipling later said he could never "get a straight statement out of him."

Difficulties with Beatty continued to grate on Rudyard's nerves, for he was a man who hated a scene, and Beatty on the other hand reveled in noisy scenes, teasing the prim and proper and stirring things up with an infectious, rowdy excitement.

"We are all a little crazy," Beatty once said of the Balestier family. "It's the only normal way to be."

Carrie did not agree. Nor did she spare Beatty a tongue-lashing when a maid caught him sneaking into the Naulakha kitchen one morning and helping himself to Josephine's malted milk.

On October 10th, Carrie wrote in her diary: "A glory of a day turned wrong by a miserable Beatty complication."

Perhaps the "miserable Beatty complication" was not the malted milk insolence, nor even his clash with Matthew Howard, whose carriage Beatty blocked from overtaking and passing on the road by slowly driving his own wagon zig-zag in front of him. Perhaps it was the persistent complaint from Beatty that the Kipling septic tank was overflowing and running off onto his land, or maybe Beatty's contention that Carrie had no right to create new formal shrub plantings on meadows to which he claimed the haying rights.

Worsening resentment made sparks fly from time to time, but which incident was so serious that Carrie ominously recorded it in her diary that day is unclear. It was doubly annoying, though, that people on Main Street and especially in the Brooks House bar were beginning to gossip about the problems between the Kiplings and Beatty.

Carrie was being blamed, called uppity and arrogant. Beatty was the hale and hearty pal to many, even though he was a drunk. Unlike his sister, he seemed to have no pretentions to be more than he really was. As for the famous Rudyard, few on Main Street would try to guess just who he was and how he might be involved in the trouble.

Kipling's fame grew, and he was sought out by admirers who flooded the Brattleboro post office with as many as two hundred letters each day. He set in motion a scheme to have the federal government establish a post office close to Naulakha, near the Putney Road, in the home of a family called Waite.

By now well-connected in Boston and New York, Kipling also had made friends with several highly placed members of President Grover Cleveland's administration. One was William Hallett Phillips, a Washington lawyer and part of the "little Washington gang" that included Henry Adams, John Hay, and Massachusetts senator Henry Cabot Lodge.

With the advice and support of Phillips, Kipling prepared a petition for a post office. It was signed by his neighbors, and he sent it to Washington.

Again the mercury drops twenty and more below zero, and the very trees swoon. . . . At night a tree's heart will break in him with a groan. According to the books, the frost has split something, but it is a fearful sound, this grunt as of a man stunned.

Leaves from a Winter Note-Book, 1895

Chapter 11

Spacious and Friendly Days

'No pen can describe the turning of the leaves—the insurrection of the tree-people against the waning year," Kipling wrote in an essay entitled "Leaves from a Winter Note-Book."

"A little maple began it, flaming blood-red of a sudden where he stood against the dark green of a pine-belt. Next morning there was an answering signal from the swamp where the sumacs grow. Three days later, the hill-sides as far as the eye could range were afire, and the roads paved with crimson and gold. Then a wet wind blew, and ruined all the uniforms of that gorgeous host; and the oaks, who had held themselves in reserve, buckled on their dull and bronzed cuirasses and stood it out stiffly to the last blown leaf, till nothing remained but pencil-shading of bare boughs, and one could see into the most private heart of the woods."

The Vermont winter of 1894–95 was approaching, and before long the roaring storms would come, able to "stop mails; wipe out all time-tables; extinguish the lamps of twenty towns, and kill a man within sight of his own doorstep. . . ."

Anticipating the majesty of winter was as thrilling as ever to Kipling, a lover of nature and its moods, but after experiencing two of them, he had acquired a certain dread. "No one who has been through . . . a blizzard as New England can produce talks lightly of the snow."

There were stories in it, and he meant to find and write them. When in Canada he had heard a young Englishman tell, "as personal experience," about a "body-snatching episode in deep snow . . . culminating in purest horror."

Fascinated, Kipling had written a draft of this story, but he had been uneasy, instinctively sensing it was "just a shade too good; too well-balanced, too slick." His daemon had told him to lay it aside, and he had left it unfinished for months. Then, having tooth trouble one day, he went to the dentist in Brattleboro, and there in the waiting room found old *Harper's* magazines from the 1850s.

"I picked up one, and read as undistractedly as the tooth permitted. There I found my tale, identical in every mark—frozen ground, frozen corpse stiff in its fur robes in the buggy. . . ." However the Englishman had come to claim that tale as

This sketch by Kipling and the accompanying note express his regrets at being unable to leave Naulakha to attend a function at a social club; the illustration suggests he is snowed in, but in fact Carrie had just been seriously burned in a mishap with their furnace.

personal experience, Rudyard thanked his daemon for not letting him publish someone else's story as his own.

Rudyard prepared himself for the hard, cold season that would lie long on Naulakha: "Frost may be looked for until the middle of May." He anticipated the exhilaration of snowshoeing in the woods with Beatty and with Will Cabot, but also was well aware of the coming isolation.

"Now in the big silence of the snow is born, perhaps, not a little of that New England conscience which her children write about. There is much time to think, and thinking is a dangerous business."

He said "conscience, fear, undigested reading" can cause restlessness, anxiety, and even the hearing of voices that instilled religious fervor, "an outpouring of the spirit" among the folk of the snowbound hills and secluded valleys. "Hate breeds as well as religion—the deep instriking hate between neighbors, that is born of a hundred little things added up, brooded over, and hatched by the stove when two or three talk together in the long evenings."

It had not come to hate between the Kiplings and Beatty, not yet, but Rudyard knew his alcoholic brother-in-law was bitterly against Carrie's advice and remonstrances. In ever-deepening financial distress, Beatty also had created hostility at Beechwood, where he sometimes went, fortified by drink, to ask for money from his grandmother. Kate, the maid there, mistrusted him, and more than once angrily hustled him out of the house while the aged Madam Balestier sobbed, despairing over the loose character of the man who had been a dear grandchild.

At the end of November, 1894, before the snow came, Arthur Conan Doyle, creator of fictional detective Sherlock Holmes, visited Rudyard at Naulakha. Conan Doyle had never met Kipling, but had known Wolcott Balestier in England.

Arriving in company with his brother, Innes, Conan Doyle was in the States on a lecture tour, in part to advance the cause of Anglo-American friendship. He wanted Kipling to tone down his public criticism of America. (Conan Doyle had earlier published a protest of Rudyard's past invective against the States.)

Specifically, Conan Doyle asked Rudyard to refrain from broadly characterizing Americans as braggarts full of hot air and tobacco juice. Just as the Englishman with a monocle was a stereotype to Americans, so the English associated dirty spittoons with stereotypical Americans.

From the start at Naulakha, these two famous writers liked each other, and spent long hours in the loggia, smoking and talking and gazing out at the leafless countryside. Conan Doyle had a particular interest in the unexplained, and they swapped eerie stories—Rudyard telling one about a Brattleboro workman who supposedly went into a trance and wrote "automatically" at the direction of some ghostly entity.

Conan Doyle brought his golf clubs to Brattleboro, which startled some locals, who knew nothing about golf and thought the clubs were medical implements. He gave Kipling golf lessons in the frost-laden meadow below the house while, as the doctor later wrote, "the New England rustics watched us." He was invited with the Kiplings to celebrate Thanksgiving at Beatty's home. Half in jest, Beatty declared that no one should have to celebrate Thanksgiving in an Englishman's house!

During this visit, the two writers surely debated the nature of Americans, for Conan Doyle had his own strong opinions, which sparked against Kipling's. Conan Doyle had written: "The race as a whole is not only the most prosperous, but the most even-tempered, tolerant, and hopeful that I have ever known. They have to meet their own problems in their own way, and I fear it is precious little sympathy they ever get from England in doing it."

The Edinburgh-born doctor was, in turn, much admired by Americans, partly because he was of Irish ancestry, which appealed to a large percentage of the population. Yet, on his lecture tour, he encountered occasional hostility because he was British—especially after a few rounds of drinks had loosened tongues around the banquet tables. More than once Conan Doyle had to sit through a speaker's harsh tirade against Britain.

Any rabble-rousing American politician who wanted attention from a crowd could easily stir it up by reviling Britain. With the presidential campaign just a year off, and the Cleveland administration in difficulty, the rhetorical bluster of prospective candidates was heating up. Far more troubling to Conan Doyle and Kipling, however, was that some Americans in high places were actually itching for an all-out war with Britain.

When he rose to reply to anti-British harangues, Conan Doyle said the isolationist America will eventually "be compelled to mix with other nations. When you do so you will find that there is only one which can at all understand your ways and aspirations. . . . That is the mother country which you are now so fond of insulting."

Kipling's friendships with kindred spirits in Washington were usually frank and blunt. John Hay once responded to Kipling's disgust with America's incessant anti-British propaganda by saying there were powerful political reasons to use mistrust of Britain as a way to influence Americans—especially the new immigrants. "America's hatred of England is the hoop around the forty-four staves of the Union," said Hay. "So, when a man comes out of the sea, we say to him: 'See that big bully over there in the east? He's England. Hate him and you're a good American.'"

During Conan Doyle's visit, Rudyard wrote "The Mother Lodge," completing these verses in only one sitting, which was unusual for him. They express his sentiments regarding the equality of all men who strive—in this case as Freemasons—for the highest of humanistic ideals. This Masonic mother lodge was one he recalled from India, its members being Sikhs, Jews, Roman Catholics, Hindus, Moslems, and ordinary Christian Englishmen, such as the speaker:

> We 'adn't good regalia,
>   An' our Lodge was old an' bare,
> But we knew the Ancient Landmarks,
>   An' we kep' 'em to a hair;
> An' lookin' on it backwards
>   It often strikes me thus,
> There ain't such things as infidels,
>   Excep', per'aps, it's us.
>
> For monthly, after Labour,
>   We'd all sit down and smoke
> (We dursn't give no banquets,
>   Lest a brother's caste were broke),
> An' man on man got talkin'
>   Religion an' the rest,
> An' every man comparin'
>   Of the God 'e knew the best.

Meeting Kipling at Naulakha would remain a treasured memory of Conan Doyle's time in New England, which he loved. Nor would he forget his tour of the Massachusetts graveyard where lay the remains of Oliver Wendell Holmes, James Russell Lowell, Francis Parkman, Henry Wadsworth Longfellow, and other great American men of letters.

When, after two days, Conan Doyle and Kipling parted as good friends, the doctor again politely admonished him to curb his criticism of Americans.

"For God's sake," Conan Doyle urged, "let's stop talking about spittoons."

Kipling did not.

Then came the shock of Robert Louis Stevenson's death on December 3rd, in Samoa. When Kipling first read the news in early December, he did not want to believe it, and wrote to a friend: "These papers lie so that I can't get at the rights of R.L.S.'s death—if indeed he be dead. It doesn't seem to me possible. It must be one of his jests and he'll 'come up with a song from the sea' while we are mourning over him."

Stevenson dying so unexpectedly sent Rudyard into such a depression that he was unable to work for days. Later that winter he was a vice president for Stevenson's memorial in Carnegie Hall, Manhattan. Now, that South Pacific voyage to meet the great novelist would never come to pass.

Around this time appeared a much-repeated news story about a young woman who supposedly arrived at Naulakha out of a December blizzard.

Author Charles Warren Stoddard, who visited Naulakha the next June, in 1895, later wrote about the story, which portrays a half-frozen woman crying for help at the door of the house while snow and wind raged. Stoddard said she was supposedly "dug out of the buffalo robes in the depths" of a rented sleigh. Placed before the blazing hearth by Carrie Kipling, she was revived by hot tea that "thawed the tears upon her icy cheeks."

To Carrie's questions, wrote Stoddard, "the stranger answered, 'I have come to interview Rudyard Kipling.'"

She was a reporter from the *New York Recorder*.

When told an interview was impossible, since Rudyard was working and would not be interrupted, the woman loudly protested, "I must interview him. I have been sent all the way from New York to interview him. . . ." The reporter was turned down and set again, "speechless with rage," in her livery sleigh.

The following week the paper's seasoned and confident Sunday editor came to Brattleboro, determined to succeed where the reporter had failed. At first, the editor sent polite notes to Naulakha, hired a sleigh to ride close to the house and tried to persuade neighbors to introduce him to Kipling. It was all much to the amusement of the community and its newspapers, which observed him trying to get that interview with Rudyard.

"But he went back to the city as empty-handed as the rest," said a newspaper.

It was said the local newspapers kept a tally of "the scribes that failed"—playing on the title of *The Light that Failed*—to see Rudyard.

Nothing daunted, the *New York Recorder* soon published a full-page "interview" with Kipling, wrote Stoddard, "and in it R.K. was made to say everything utterable or unutterable that was calculated to put him in the most unfavorable light before the public."

Thus the story circulated widely about the poor woman bravely arriving at Naulakha in a terrible December snowstorm and being ruthlessly thrown out again. She may indeed have been turned away, but it could not have been during a blizzard, for in a letter Rudyard sent to New England writer Sarah Orne Jewett on December 24th, he said, "No snow—the roads like iron—and the thermometer nearly zero. . . ."

On December 30th, Rudyard wrote his entry in Carrie's diary: "C tots up the books and finds I have this year earned $25,000–£5,000. Not exactly a bad record. Not that mine be the praise, but C. deserves it all."

At this time, he was receiving much public adulation for the first *Jungle Book*, including a letter from New England author Edward Everett Hale, famous for his short story "The Man Without a Country." Kipling replied: "Praise from you is praise to be proud of and henceforward I shall look upon the *Jungle Book* with respect."

The second *Jungle Book* was to be published later in 1895, and Rudyard was working on the last story, entitled "The Spring Running."

On January 14th Carrie endured a painful and frightening accident, as her face was scorched when she opened the woodburning furnace and flames shot out, even singeing her eyebrows. Never very robust to begin with, the badly shaken Carrie was laid up in her room for days, her face oiled and swathed with cotton bandages. The Kiplings saw no company in the next few weeks other than Dr. Conland, who advised them to go away that spring so Carrie could rest, for the injuries would be slow in healing.

Conland also advised Rudyard to do something to cheer her up. She was bearing the burden of Beatty's animosity as well as suffering from her injury. Conland hinted that Rudyard buy a new team of carriage horses, for Carrie loved to drive, and Rod and Rick were increasingly troublesome. Kipling soon bought Nip and Tuck, a handsome pair of well-trained Morgans, from Beatty for $650— a sum that kept him solvent.

Carrie's eyes pained her when she read, but she was eager to drive the horses and took them for daily spins, her face bandaged closely so that only one eye could see. Beside her sat Rudyard, full of anxiety as they dashed along. Carrie soon loved these two horses so much that Kipling referred to them in a letter as the "Sacred Pair." He even bought her a new carriage, naming it the "More Sacred Phaeton," described as "blood red . . . with basket sides and wings and *such* a rumble."

Carrie slowly recovered, but her soft brown hair turned prematurely gray, continuing to lose its color until in a matter of weeks it was completely white.
In February, Kipling publicly complained about the ongoing Brattleboro trolley developments. He wrote to local attorney Edgar W. Stoddard, who represented op-

Carrie poses in their carriage as driver Matthew Howard looks on.

position to the line, saying if the proposed trolley went into operation, he would be cut off from the Brattleboro train station and his usual shopping places.

Kipling said "no man who has had experience of trollies and their workings would willingly risk the lives of his family or his horses by exposing them to the daily chances of accident from direct collision with the cars, from the fallen wires or from runaways."

If the trolley were built, he might altogether stop coming to Brattleboro on business and would use a station farther up the line instead. He even wrote some derogatory verses calling Brattleboro "Crosby's Dump," after one Edward Crosby, president of the Brattleboro Street Railway Company.

The project moved forward despite Rudyard's objections.

In his mind just then were plans for another trip to Bombay that fall, and he proposed to *Cosmopolitan Magazine* that he write letters of travel. Clearly, he was already reluctant to spend the next winter in Vermont.

In a letter to Charles Eliot Norton, he complained of "knife-edged cold, and a cloudless sky, a sun grinning like a skull, and a wind that ripped the bones off you. . . . But our house has been singing like a ship brought up in the wind's eye and the old maple has been creaking and there are five or six feet of snow generally about the place and at least ten in the air."

He wrote a limerick about the northeastern winter for a fifteen-year-old writer in Scotland, saying she could publish it in a children's magazine she edited:

> *There was a small boy in Quebec*
> *Who was buried in snow to the neck.*
> *When they asked:— "Are you friz?"*
> *He replied:— "Yes I is,*
> *"But we don't call this cold in Quebec."*

That April, to get away from Vermont's mud season and following the orders of Dr. Conland to give Carrie a change of scene, the Kiplings went to Washington for a few weeks.

Rudyard visited friends among the long-time American diplomats and bureaucrats, and for the most part it was a delightful time. He resumed his acquaintance with Theodore Roosevelt, then a Civil Service commissioner. They had first met in New York, when Roosevelt was police commissioner there and Kipling had asked a mutual acquaintance for an introduction.

The straight-talking, good-humored Roosevelt was the antidote to a disheartening tour Kipling made of Congress. Rudyard found the raucous House of Representatives a distressingly undignified spectacle, rowdy and rude and rife with those dirty spittoons. He was flabbergasted by the wife of Henry Cabot Lodge, who invited him to an anti-English speech her husband was about to make to the Senate. She said cheerfully that it would be great fun to hear her husband "twist the lion's tail."

Rudyard declined to attend.

After meeting President Cleveland and several cabinet members in the White House, Kipling went back to the hotel to tell Carrie he was utterly disgusted by them. She wrote in her diary that he said it was "awful, inexpressible; incredible; a colossal agglomeration of reeking bounders; it made him very sorrowful."

Not so when it came to Teddy Roosevelt, though the two of them teased and scolded and joked with each other about the swollen British empire and the ruthless course of American expansion. Kipling later recalled their conversations: "I never got over the wonder of how a people, who, having extirpated the aboriginals of their continent more completely than any modern race has ever done, honestly believed that they were a godly little New England community, setting examples to brutal mankind."

While browsing with Roosevelt in the Smithsonian Institution, Kipling tried to explain "this wonder," and Roosevelt "made the glass cases of Indian relics shake with his rebuttals." When Rudyard asked Roosevelt how, when Americans were so opposed to taxation, the States could ever build a strong navy, the gleeful answer was, "Out of you!" meaning, out of the widespread American distrust of England.

Kipling later said, "But those were great and spacious and friendly days in Washington which—politics apart—Allah had not deprived of a sense of humor; and the food was a thing to dream of."

Gray Brother brings news to Mowgli, from "Tiger! Tiger!" in *The Jungle Books.*
Illustrator: W.H. Drake

Ere yet we loose the legions—
  Ere yet we draw the blade,
Jehovah of the Thunders,
  Lord God of Battles, aid!

Hymn Before Action, 1896

Chapter 12

Quarrels

By late 1895, there was a lively traffic around the world in Rudyard Kipling ephemera, including letters, original manuscripts, and anything with his signature on it.

Some letters sent to Rudyard were exclusively intended to elicit a signed reply which then could be sold. In one case, a writer sent Kipling a quarter, saying if Rudyard was indeed paid that much per word, would he sell one for the enclosed quarter?

"Kip did," recalled Dave Carey, the stationmaster at Brattleboro, who saw him often in the depot. "He wrote 'Thanks' on the letter and mailed it back."

It said something about the financially pressed Beatty that he refrained from selling valuable gifts Rudyard had given him—the manuscript of an early *Jungle Books* story and the unpublished poem to Marjorie—as well as several Kipling letters he owned.

In part to foil speculators who bought and sold Kipling's signature, but mostly to benefit her favorite charity, Carrie organized a plan to sell autographs at two dollars and fifty cents each, the money to be paid to the Fresh Air Fund. The plan was sponsored by the *New York Herald*, and more than 200 signatures were sold, raising cash for the Fund, which sent poor city children into the country for vacations. Soon, however, there came loud criticism from those who sneered that it was just a publicity gimmick. Carrie was deeply hurt and cancelled the scheme.

Later that spring, Rudyard related in a letter how the road a mile down the hill collapsed in a heavy rain, and he and Carrie "went down to repair it in deep mud with sticks and boughs and unmitigated dirt. It's nice to make mud pies always but when you feel you are doing the community a service and can get filthy without any one to say 'don't' you revel in it."

He also wrote to Lucius Tuttle, president of the Boston and Maine Railroad, which crossed an iron girder bridge over the West River as it entered the Connecticut north of Brattleboro. Kipling said trains on the railroad bridge appeared

Three Bridges Brattleboro Vt.

Buggy and wagon drivers had anxious moments at this covered bridge north of Brattleboro when their horses were terrified by the sudden noisy passing of a train; Kipling persuaded the railroad to sound warning whistles, giving drivers time to stop before entering the bridge.

suddenly and without warning, terrifying the teams pulling carriages or wagons across the adjacent covered bridge.

"Thus, when one is surprised by a train while driving in the covered bridge the situation is trying to the nerves of even the steadiest horse, who is close to and a little below a deafening clamour, and is unable to see where it comes from."

To prevent stampeding the horses, Kipling suggested trains should whistle as they approached, and in this way drivers with buggies or wagons would be warned to wait before attempting to cross the covered bridge. Tuttle politely accepted the suggestion, and the trains were instructed from then on to sound a warning whistle.

Kipling's quiet community service, such as repairing washed-out roads and persuading railroads to change their ways, went virtually unknown, but gave him personal satisfaction. It was a far cry from publicly selling autographs for charity.

By now, Carrie forbade any unauthorized scrap of Rudyard's work, his signature, or even casual writing to leave the premises. Thus she meant to stem the traffic in Kipling ephemera—which at one point included an American publisher buying all the office files of the *Pioneer* in India in order to search them for anything by Kipling that was publishable and uncopyrighted.

Carrie despised anyone taking advantage of her husband or making a profit from selling his personal items. If the verse he wrote did not please him, it went into the trash to be burned rather than allow any chance of it being recovered and sold or published. Even when he entertained close friends with his spontaneous versifying—as often he did—no one was permitted to make notes, no matter how clever or frivolous the verse might be.

When Carrie learned that his letters and even his signed personal checks were being bought and sold for the autograph, she undertook to stop it. She became the only one to sign checks, and any less-personal correspondence from Rudyard was dictated to her and left unsigned.

After all the years of pirated editions and frequent invasions of their privacy, the Kiplings obsessively fought to foil those who would profit, without authorization, from Rudyard's popular appeal. They did this against an overwhelming tide of interest in anything belonging to him.

Although he had a deeply spiritual nature, Kipling seldom went to Sunday worship services (Carrie attended the local Episcopalian church). Molly Cabot said Rudyard liked to write hymns on Sundays, and often visited on Mondays to let her hear them. Then they were immediately burned.

Others said Kipling liked best to spend the Sabbath at the house of Walter H. Childs, where they were joined by Dr. Conland. While their families were at church, according to C. F. Childs, the son of Walter Childs, they would sit for an hour around the dining room table, talking over a glass of whisky and soda. A favorite subject was the hereafter, which they all apparently doubted existed in the conventional sense. According to C. F. Childs, they said if the hereafter did exist, then the first one who died would send some sign to the others to prove there was, indeed, a hereafter.

As for disembodied daemons and muses, Rudyard had no doubts.

"I have this week finished the last of the new Jungle book with the words 'and this is to be the last of the Mowgli tales because there are no more to be told.' "

Kipling wrote this in a June 18th letter to Mary Mapes Dodge of *St. Nicholas Magazine*. Years later, he said, "My Daemon was with me in *The Jungle Books* . . . and I took good care to walk delicately, lest he should withdraw." He went on to say that a writer who knows the muse "is in charge" should "not try to think consciously. Drift, wait, and obey."

In company with creatures of *The Jungle Books,* Mowgli carries the hide of the tiger, Shere Khan, whom the wolf-boy has killed to avoid being killed.

Kipling obeyed, and when the Mowgli stories came to an end it was "with almost the water-hammer click of a tap turned off." After completing "The Spring Running" in March, 1895, *The Jungle Books* were finished.

"Now we must try new things," he told Mrs. Dodge. He especially wanted to write about a new kind of woman, one less delicate, less frilly, more independent—much like American women he had met, perhaps even like Carrie.

First, there was something else to face, however, and it often cost him the composure needed to write in peace: Beatty and Carrie were hotly disputing the terms of the contract for the new tennis court, which Beatty had just finished. It was apparent he had not paid all the suppliers with the funds Carrie had given him specifically for that purpose.

By now, Beatty was no longer Rudyard's right-hand man, that place being taken by Matthew Howard, who not only was excellent with the horses, but also enjoyed planting trees and shrubs and carrying out the many tasks of maintaining the Naulakha estate. There now was a carriage house, with Howard's family quarters above it, and an ice house, just built.

Because of Beatty's increasingly surly attitude, Rudyard and Carrie deeply regretted their original agreement allowing him free run of the property. Beatty had the right to cross their land at will, and to take the hay off the fields as he saw fit. There were no more family outings to Lake Raponda these days, and even Marjorie and Josephine seldom played together any more. Old hurts ached again, including the memory of Carrie's frigid behavior to Mai back in 1889, when Carrie thought Beatty needed reining in, and resented it that his new wife did not agree.

Beatty was still the talk of Brattleboro, charging faster than the speed limit across the West River covered bridge in a buckboard drawn by a pair of ponies, and followed at a distance by a mob of the fox terriers he bred. He was a familiar sight, skidding up to the Brooks House and jumping down to enter the cellar bar. In a few moments his dogs would appear, one by one, and sit in a crowd around the buckboard, waiting for the dash homeward.

Beatty's once-hearty companionship with Rudyard was eroded by the constant clashes with Carrie. Rudyard was caught in the middle, but in fact his own personality also went head-to-head with his brother-in-law's. Perhaps, they were too much alike: both enjoyed being the center of attention, leading the conversation, and aggressively debating anything from politics to literature to religion. Each was extremely well read, holding strong opinions, and capable of flashing at an opponent's weak point with devastating wit or irresistible cunning.

Both loved fun and were equally magnetic and charming, but they were taking sharply divergent paths through the world. Rudyard was living the cultured, reserved life that depended on Carrie for the security, peace, and quiet his writing required. Beatty, on the other hand, sought boisterously high times wherever he could find them, without a care for tomorrow, though all the while he was sinking financially.

As for the point of view of Vermont's onlookers, Kipling was considered an aloof, rich Britisher, cold and superior, with a social-climbing wife; Beatty was the gay-blade-about-town, the good fellow unfailingly kind to friends and, unlike Carrie, always willing to entertain unexpected guests or to put an extra plate on the table. More than one neighbor owed Beatty favors that were difficult to match, such as getting an ill wife to the doctor on a stormy night, or rescuing cattle and horses trapped in snowdrifts.

Where Kipling was proper and polite, Beatty was a roaring, volcanic braggart erupting with oaths. If Beatty's conversation was full of "rasping, gleeful" profanity at which few took offense, then Rudyard by contrast appeared tight lipped, and seemed, as one writer said, "monosyllabically frigid" to strangers. Kipling was openly envied for his astounding professional triumphs, and Beatty was envied by many for his incomparable enthusiasm for life.

Carrie well loved her younger brother, but she dreaded that he would one day become a bankrupt, leaving his wife and daughter destitute and shaming the Balestier name.

At one time, Rudyard had hopes of creating in Brattleboro a circle of acquaintances to suit his and Carrie's tastes, but this ambition was fading. He later wrote in his autobiography that "a promising scheme for a Country Club had to be abandoned because many men who would by right belong to it could not be trusted with a full whisky bottle. On the farms, of course, men drank cider, of various strengths, and sometimes achieved almost maniacal forms of drunkenness."

Beatty surely was included in this category.

Though his relationship with Beatty was fast deteriorating, Rudyard had good local friends, including Dr. Conland, Walter Childs, the elderly former governor Frederick Holbrook, John Bliss, and Will and Molly Cabot. Stationmaster Dave Carey always enjoyed listening to him talk at the train station, saying "Kip" wrote just as he spoke. Kipling once said to Carey that the females of a race were more dangerous than the males; years later Carey told a writer: "I recalled that, long after, when I read his poetry about 'The Female of the Species.' It was like hearing Kip say it all over again."

The farmers near Naulakha were willing to sign Rudyard's petition for a post office to be established at the home of Mrs. Anna F. Waite, who was to be postmistress. He told William Hallett Phillips, the Washington lawyer, he should have seen him "getting solid with [the farmers] on the lee side of barns. I find I have in me unsuspecting powers of softening the Vermonter and not suffering him to be ferocious."

The post office, designated as "Waite," was granted late that spring, largely because of Phillips's intercession with President Cleveland.

Kipling thanked Phillips: "It's the first time in my life that I ever felt dripping with the milk of human kindness to all the members of a Government Department (as a journalist in India of course I fought 'em on principle) and I like the experience."

By June 19th, Kipling was writing on his return address: Naulakha, Waite's, via Brattleboro, Vermont. Later, he sent hundreds of printed postcards reading: "Please note change of address from Brattleboro, Vt., to WAITE, Windham County, Vermont. Be careful not to omit name of county. Rudyard Kipling."

The despised trolley line was going through on Main Street, but at least Rudyard had his own post office, and next he hoped for a train depot and a country store at Waite's. "After which comes the telegraph freight and express agency." He joked about even running for governor. In the meantime, there was lots of work to be done around Naulakha: building stone walls, constantly maintaining the touchy pump that supplied their water, and creating landscaped gardens.

Then Carrie and Beatty had a disastrous blowup over her plans for landscaping the hayfield. The crisis occurred early in July, 1895, when the Kiplings were visiting the Balestiers at Maplewood. In this house they were surrounded by mementos of Carrie's maternal grandfather, Peshine Smith, who had been advisor to the Japanese Mikado. A magnificent ceremonial sword hanging over the brick mantlepiece was the most imposing. There, too, was Beatty's fine library, which showed his wide-ranging and powerful intellect; he owned a prized collection of fine engravings, and in a place of honor were signed copies of Kipling books.

Frederic Van de Water wrote about Beatty's side of this argument: Beatty claimed to have sold the mowing to the Kiplings for a dollar, declaring "Hell, I don't care about the property as a building site. All I want off it is hay for my stock. You agree to let me keep on mowing it, and you can have it."

As the years passed, however, Beatty came to so resent Carrie's behavior that he bridled at her plans for turning part of the meadow into formal gardens.

He is quoted by Van de Water as saying, "And then, by God, I heard that Caroline had a landscape architect up and was going to turn that mowing into a formal garden. I didn't believe it but when they came one night to dinner at my house, I asked about it and Caroline said it was true. I told her:

"'You're in my house; you're my guest but by Christ, once you've left it, I'll never speak to you again as long as I live.'"

Van de Water said brother and sister quarreled furiously, while Rudyard sat in silence. They all knew the argument truly was not about a haymow or a formal garden, and when the Kiplings left Maplewood, it appeared they and Beatty were finished for good. This wretchedness happened just when Carrie learned she was pregnant again.

A few days later, on July 6th, Rudyard and Carrie departed for a brief visit to England, leaving Josephine in the care of her grandmother, Anna Balestier, at the Fairview Inn, East Gloucester, Massachusetts.

They were heartsick over the complications at Naulakha, but made the best of their trip. It was further troubling that the Cleveland administration was challenging the British government over a long-simmering minor border dispute between British Guiana and Venezuela. While Kipling was in England, the American secretary of state made an extremely rude reply to the British offer of settlement terms. The British attitude toward the States then hardened, and the situation began moving toward a major collision.

In the States, hawks were extolling the moral and spiritual benefits of war, saying it "is not the great evil that it is painted," calling war "an educator," necessary for the perpetuation of patriotism, and a means by which to "clear the atmosphere and stamp out the growth of socialism and anarchy, discontent and sectional prejudice that is gaining a foothold in this nation."

Massachusetts senator Lodge, one of Rudyard's acquaintances in the "little Washington gang," rattled the saber harder than anyone. Lodge charged Britain with trying to get hold of rich Venezuelan mining regions in violation of the 1823 Monroe Doctrine, which asserted there should be no further European colonization in the Americas.

Rudyard steamed when he read the American government's statement that the United States "is practically sovereign on [the South American] continent. . . . because . . . its infinite resources combined with its isolated position render it master of the situation, and practically invulnerable as against any or all powers."

In spite of politics, the visit to England was good, for it was always a pleasure to see Lockwood and Alice Kipling. Lockwood was busy making bas relief sculptures to be photographed as illustrations for the *Second Jungle Book*, and this was a source of much satisfaction to Rudyard.

Upon his return to Naulakha later that summer, Rudyard found the country abuzz with speculation about what would happen next between the States and Britain. It galled him to hear Americans boast about their military power, and he was especially appalled when friends treated the horrors of war so lightly.

If Rudyard tried to explain his concern, they often grinned and said, "Oh, that's because you're afraid." He had seen "one or two ugly sights" in his days on the frontier in India and knew what could come of war. He was short-tempered with those who took lightly the prospects of a war between America and Britain.

One afternoon at Naulakha, during a luncheon with Molly Cabot and other friends, the conversation turned to the Venezuelan troubles. Molly remarked flippantly that she knew little about any of it. Rudyard said gravely that it was no small matter, for the British Navy's "Great White Squadron" could methodically destroy all the major American cities along the East Coast in a matter of days.

When Molly lightly replied that she believed no navy could possibly do that, Kipling's frayed nerves gave way and he got up abruptly from the table and left the room. Molly was expressing what Rudyard believed was the dangerous ignorance of so many Americans about the trouble that was brewing. He had to walk alone in the woods to calm himself.

Matters were turning out much worse than he had expected. The Venezuelan issue was not just table conversation or a political toy, for it could lead to full-scale war between his chosen home country and his native land. If there was war, where would he go? What about Carrie and Jo and the coming baby? He might have to leave them here and go north to Canada, but war would surely come there if the Americans invaded the undefended border. Or he could return to England. One way or the other, he was determined to back the British.

In Kipling's thoughts were verses which he prayed he never would have to publish: "Hymn Before Action" was a warning to the Americans, a call to arms for the British.

> *The earth is full of anger,*
> > *The seas are dark with wrath,*
> *The Nations in their harness*
> > *Go up against our path:*
> *Ere yet we loose the legions—*
> > *Ere yet we draw the blade,*
> *Jehovah of the Thunders,*
> > *Lord God of Battles, aid!*
>
> * * *
>
> *E'en now their vanguard gathers,*
> > *E'en now we face the fray—*
> *As Thou didst help our fathers,*
> > *Help Thou our host today.*
> *Fulfilled of signs and wonders,*
> > *In life, in death made clear—*
> *Jehovah of the Thunders,*
> > *Lord God of Battles, hear!*

"And so ends our fourth and best year. The Lord has been good to us beyond telling, and we have taken delight in all the days of our life."

Rudyard Kipling's comment in Carrie Kipling's diary, December 31, 1895

Chapter 13

If Trouble Comes

In the fall of 1895, the Naulakha rose garden with its flagstone walk was a favorite place for Rudyard to walk and smoke and think. There was much to ponder in these turbulent days. For all that America posed problems, Rudyard was increasingly attached to Vermont, and well he knew it. On his triumphant visit to England, he even had been told he had picked up an American accent.

Things here by now were familiar, homelike. The distant gray-blue peak of Mount Monadnock, seen from Naulakha, was a dependable weather prophet to Rudyard: when the mountain was clearly visible, the weather would be good; when Monadnock was capped with clouds, rain was certain.

Molly Cabot asked him if he would be in England that coming spring, and he replied, "What? Leave Vermont when the anemones are in bloom? Never!" He told her he could not be happy in England, and that Naulakha was the ideal place for him to create. He and Carrie did have thoughts of building a seaside vacation house on the south coast of England, but had not yet put plans into effect.

Kipling wrote to family in England that little Jo was a real American, "who trots at our heels and gives orders." In the morning, she fed acorns to the two pigs, "Bubble" and "Squeak," before going to the stable for her daily horseback ride. She was a delightful and beautiful fair-haired child, who enjoyed the holiday visits of Carrie's mother from New York. "I can hear her from time to time shouting:—'Tum along, Gwan muvver!'"

Kipling loved to watch her dart through the rose garden, and run through long grass as he and Carrie went for walks with her up the side of the hill. There they sat above the house and enjoyed the views. The inspiration of these walks (and of the wildflowers Rudyard loved so) brought out the verses "The Flowers." It was a song to those English who had settled in homes around the world—homes with new birds and flowers and land to love, homes which held them and caused such turbulence when homesickness for England came upon them.

Buy my English posies!
Ye that have your own
Buy them for a brother's sake
Overseas, alone!
Weed ye trample underfoot
Floods his heart abrim—
Bird ye never heeded,
Oh, she calls his dead to him!

Kipling's work progressed in a new and fresh way, as he was moved by a dream to write the ethereal tale "The Brushwood Boy" about an ideal young English officer whose own dreams are so unsettling, especially when they come true.

Several other important stories came out of this period, eventually to be collected in the volume entitled *The Day's Work*. These included "The Devil and the Deep Sea," "The Ship that Found Herself," and the story about that new woman, "William the Conqueror."

This last tale describes an Englishwoman in India, struggling to save people in a famine. She has a man's name and boyish attributes, though she is also beautiful and falls in love with an idealistic, self-sacrificing civil servant as they distribute food to starving children. Carrie thought this modern heroine "came out stunningly."

Rudyard also was thinking back on his youth at Westward Ho! and planning to work up a "boy's book and pitch the scene there." This would become *Stalky and Co.* Now and again he tried to turn to that long novel about the British boy living like a native in India, playing the dual roles of a British spy and a companion of a mendicant monk searching for the river of eternal life. The story still would not come clear to Kipling, and he set it aside "to be smoked over with the Pater."

That fall the Kipling family traveled northward a few hours by rail to visit the Newbury, New Hampshire, second home of diplomat John Hay, who in a year would become ambassador to Britain in the McKinley administration. There was much fun, and when Kipling "rattled off the frame-work of about forty stories," Hay wondered, "How a man can keep up so intense an intellectual life without going to Bedlam is amazing."

Unlike Cleveland's picked men, Hay was no anti-British warmonger, but he was not as yet in a political position to affect the belligerent course of the U.S. government.

The almost comic-farce Venezuelan issue steamed onward. The absurd, but increasingly possible, prospect of war between England and America gnawed at Kipling.

He was always defensive whenever Britain was insulted by anyone but him—just as he quickly spoke up for America when a Britisher insulted her. Now, the windbag bravado coming from too many American politicians infuriated him, instilling a deep and unmitigated anger.

One former Texas congressman declared the ongoing policy of defying and insulting the British a "winner" in light of America's "internal ills." The fellow declared that "one cannon shot across the bow of a British boat" would be the medicine to cure the "anarchistic, socialistic and populistic boil" in the nation.

The Monroe Doctrine was waved in the face of the British government, and one senator said God was the Doctrine's author.

It all simmered and mingled with the Beatty troubles, and also with another annoying failure of the Kipling water pump. Although by now the families at Naulakha and Maplewood were conversing only through written notes, the Kiplings were embarrassingly obliged to draw water from Beatty's well until the artesian well produced again.

Even attempts at reconciliation by the visiting Anna Balestier could not soften her son Beatty's anger with her daughter Carrie. As for his opinion of Rudyard, Beatty was not irreconcilably set against him, for it was a Balestier family dispute. Still, he said, "Kip talked too much!"

Early that October, Rudyard was briefly distracted by an enjoyable visit from young Owen Wister, an up-and-coming novelist and a close friend of Teddy Roosevelt's. Wister would soon write his masterpiece, *The Virginian,* perhaps the first true-to-life western novel about a realistic and extremely appealing cowboy hero.

Whatever emotions Kipling felt, he was obviously under stress by early November. Where, in his first winter, he had declared the clear air of Vermont to be invigorating, he now was suffering from the chilly weather. For the first time in ages, he and Carrie came "down with that most destroying sort of cold—a dull sobbled thing that is going the rounds. As neither of us look for this from year's end to year's end we are the more angry."

When Indian summer arrived in mid-November, he said it would be "the most perfect season of the year if the days were not shortened." Soon he was writing, "It is snowing hard in this part of the world (where our winters are long and cold) and if I wasn't eaten up with a cold in the head I'd write you a longer letter."

Even Josephine had a cold, and that was most troubling of all in a day when the risk of fatal pneumonia was extreme. When Rudyard heard of a neighbor's child dying, he remarked that if he ever lost his Josephine he feared he could not possibly bear it.

There were satisfactions, too, in this difficult period, including a visit from E. Kay Robinson, a longtime friend and Kipling's former editor from newspaper days in India. Robinson was touring America, and he brought Rudyard the delightful news that two railway stations in the Midwest had been named after him, one Rudyard and the other Kipling. They were on the Minneapolis, St. Paul, and Sault Ste. Marie line, both in Michigan's upper peninsula.

"This immensely flatters my vanity," Kipling wrote to the president of the railroad. "I shall take deep interest in their welfares."

He understood the stop called Rudyard already had a post office, but "Please encourage the development of 'Kipling.' Give him an express and telegraph office, and a new water-tank, and if ever he has a restaurant let it be known for the best coffee on the line."

He wrote verses entitled "The Michigan Twins":

> *Wise is the child who knows his sire,*
> *The ancient proverb ran.*
> *But wiser far the man who knows*
> *How, where and when his offspring grows,*
> *For who the mischief would suppose*
> *I've sons in Michigan?*
> *Yet I am saved from midnight ills*
> *That warp the soul of man.*
> *They do not make me walk the floor,*
> *Nor hammer at the doctor's door;*
> *They deal in wheat and iron ore,*
> *My sons in Michigan.*
> *O tourist in the Pullman car*
> *(By Cook's or Raymond's plan)*
> *Forgive a partial parent's view*
> *But maybe you have children too—*
> *So let me introduce to you*
> *My sons in Michigan.*

Extremely important at this time was the first visit of Scribners editor Frank Nelson Doubleday, who came to open negotiations for his company to produce a complete edition of Kipling's work.

Though the Kiplings were normally suspicious of publishers and were not at first very warm to Doubleday, he quickly won their hearts and began a lifelong friendship. A large and handsome young man with an open face and cheerful nature, Doubleday's initials, "F. N. D.," sounded like the Turkish title of honor, "effendi." He soon became known to the Kiplings as "Beloved Effendi."

In these days Kipling corresponded happily with Joel Chandler Harris, creator of the immensely popular Uncle Remus stories. They admired each other, and their friendship meant much to Kipling, whose boyhood was spent deep in the Brer Rabbit stories. He wrote to Harris:

"I wonder if you could realize how Uncle Remus and his sayings and the sayings of the noble beasties ran like wild fire through an English public school when I was about fifteen."

Rudyard and his schoolmates lived and breathed Harris's stories, and even when they were reunited as soldiers, writers, and government officials in India, "we found ourselves quoting whole pages of Uncle Remus that had got mixed in with the fabric of the old school life."

The two authors compared their Indian and African-American folktale characters and were amazed by how they could find a match for almost every one. On the mantelpiece and bookshelf in Kipling's Naulakha study were plaster figures of *Jungle Book* characters, treasured gifts to him from Harris.

Another diversion that November was a visit by Elizabeth Bacon Custer, widow of the late Gen. George Armstrong Custer, who two decades earlier had been defeated and killed by Indians at the Little Big Horn. Mrs. Custer was on a lecture tour and stayed with the Kiplings for a night before delivering her talk the next day in Brattleboro.

When, that fall, the New York publishing firm of G.W. Dillingham released *Out of India,* an unauthorized collection of Kipling's early uncopyrighted work, Rudyard was "sick at my stomach" with disgust and frustration. He wrote a letter to the editors of leading publications saying he had nothing to do with this "common fake." It was even more maddening that Dillingham added new verse headings to the letters and sketches, as if Kipling himself had written them.

In December, Rudyard told a New York acquaintance, "If, as Mr. Cleveland seems to think, there is going to be war and you see me coming round the 14th Street curve on a curvetting cable-car with a drawn sword in my hand you'll know that I'm looking for G.W. Dillingham."

In his annual message to Congress—still boosting for votes—President Cleveland again warned Britain against "the enlargement of the area of British Guiana in derogation of the rights and against the will of Venezuela." He then asked Congress to create a commission, which he would appoint, to investigate the disputed boundary. He added that the U.S. would use "every means in its power" to thwart British transgressions.

Many Americans wholeheartedly and loudly agreed. One American business publication said the United States must resist the British even if it led to "blood and iron." The British agreed to arbitration in the South American border dispute, but there was as yet no guarantee of a peaceful solution.

In fact, Britain was not in a strong position just then, since she had no major ally in the world. Serious troubles were brewing with the French in Africa, and armed, rebellious Boers (white farmers) in South Africa were openly supported by the Germans in a longstanding, worsening conflict with the British colonial administration.

Every passing day brought the crisis between England and America closer to a climax, and also brought Carrie closer to giving birth. In part because of Carrie's pregnancy (she was due in February) the projected journey back to India that winter was impossible.

By the end of December plans were in the wind to go to England that summer or autumn "for some long time," Rudyard told an English friend, adding, "so despair not if someday you see the wife and me coming over the hills very hungry with trunks in a cart."

He told this friend, who had just married: "If marriage makes your life to you one half as good and wholesome as it has made mine to me, you'll be blessed: and I wish all good on you and yours and your house for many generations."

Kipling was thinking of slowing down his writing production, and said, "I hope to go into dry-dock for a year or two . . . and adjust my notions of things generally." He was so uneasy about what might happen politically that he still seriously contemplated how to get out of America by himself. Carrie could not go away while so near to term, but Rudyard worried that if there were an all-out war, he might be in danger, attacked by a mob or arrested as an enemy alien.

That Christmas he wrote to Charles Eliot Norton: "I feel regularly upset and bewildered about it—as if I had been aimed at with a decanter across a friendly dinner table. But I can only pray that it will come out right."

He told Norton: "I seem to be between two barrels like a pheasant. If the American mine is sprung it means dirt and slush and ultimately death either across the Canada border or in some disemboweled gunboat off Cape Hatteras. If the German dynamite is exploded equally it means slaughter and most probably on the high seas. In both cases I am armed with nothing more efficient than a notebook, a stylographic pen and a pair of opera glasses. Whether or no, anyway and inevitably, C. will be confined within the next three or five weeks and till that time I am tied here by the leg."

If Rudyard must suddenly leave the country, he had "arranged things so that C. ought not to starve: and she has the house and my copyrights to boot. You see it is obviously absurd of me to sit still and go on singing from a safe place while the men I know are in the crown of it: and it may be that when I am closer to the scene of action I may be able to help with a little song or two in the intervals of special correspondence. But it is borne in upon me by the inner eye that if trouble comes I shan't live to see it out."

He was resigned to leaving the States before long.

"All these things fill me with a deep love for Mr. Cleveland who is responsible for the letting in of the waters. I permit myself, however, to cherish the hope that the row or rows may be delayed till May when I can hope to pick up C. and the children (*D.V.*) and take 'em to England. I shan't mind so much then: but whether it be peace or war, this folly puts an end to my wholesome life here: and to me that is the saddest part of it. We must begin again from the beginning else-where and pretend that we are only anxious to let the house for a year or two. It's hard enough God knows but I should be a fool if after full warning I risked my own people's happiness and comfort in a hostile country."

He said five generations of Americans being taught to hate England "and easy talk of killing on slight provocation" had injured the people's "moral insides."

"All the same the American situation is intensely comic in a sombre and devilish sort of way. I have the melancholy satisfaction of saying to myself:—'I told you so' about a hundred times a day: but it seems to me best not to say or write or sing a word publicly—yet.

"As to the German business I don't care a continental. It will wake up the colonies and teach us to keep our powder dry. But the American thing makes me sick and sore and sorry to my heart's core. People can say what they please. There was a much more genuine absence of hostility on the English side than there was on the American: and I do sincerely believe that the American interior press is re-sponsible for the cherishing of that hostile feeling.

"But this is a grossly personal view of the matter and a man with a wife and child and another baby expected may be excused for a certain amount of selfishness." He closed with: "I and mine are always affectionately yours. No war or series of wars could make any difference in that, thank God. If Grover doesn't know when he has a good friend, I do. Ever yours affectionately, Ruddy."

As for the difficulties with Beatty, in a letter to their friend Sallie Norton, daughter of Charles Eliot Norton, Rudyard conceded that matters were worse than ever: "It is all most dolefully true, and having said that one feels as if there ought to be some way out of it—the consequences, I mean. I'm going to hope hard for the very best. C. is wonderfully well, considering things, and I'm proud of her."

". . . and now I am the captive of your bow and spear. I'm not kicking at that. . . . I don't tag after our consul when he comes around, expecting the American Eagle to lift me out o' this by the slack of my pants. No, sir! If a Britisher went into Indian Territory and shot up his surroundings with a Colt automatic (not that she's any sort of weapon, but I take her for an illustration), he'd be strung up quicker'n a snowflake 'ud melt in hell. No ambassador of yours 'ud save him."

Laughton G. Zigler, a fictional American armaments inventor captured by the British in the Boer War, as he meets the narrator in Kipling's story "The Captive," 1901

Chapter 14

The Native Born

By early 1896, Rudyard was hungrily collecting information for his novel to be set in the world of New England cod-fishing. He pressed James Conland for all he was worth, even learning from the doctor how to gut fish the way the fishermen did it.

Kipling also corresponded with Frederick N. Finney, a railroad executive who answered questions for the novel, including working out the fastest railway route from California to Boston. In these letters to Finney Rudyard told about the story "An Error in the Fourth Dimension," saying it was based on the concept that there is "in every land a dimension in which no one except a lawful native of the land can move without violent collisions."

For Kipling, the gathering clouds of war between Britain and the United States were exposing his own vulnerability to those same collisions.

Asked by Washington friend William Hallett Phillips to take a trip to Yellowstone National Park in the Rockies, he refused, saying, "I can't say I feel very festive. This damned Venezuelan rot has made me sick to my heart. It may be fine and picturesque and patriotic and all the rest of it but it has done America a damage it will take her fifty years to recover from, in the eyes of the civilized world."

He was sick at heart, too, about the sorry conflict with Beatty. The Kiplings and Balestiers had scarcely communicated after the blowup back in July. Since then, Beatty had earned nothing from the Kiplings, and he was failing financially. At the same time, Rudyard's fortunes soared, as did his reputation around the world. This certainly could have made Beatty all the more frustrated.

Kipling later said he did not want the rift, but Beatty "dropped me." At first, he had gone to Beatty's house "to continue as if nothing had happened," but Beatty refused to speak to him. Life was increasingly unhappy on that Vermont hillside, as each day the Kiplings had to pass in sight of Maplewood to get down to the post office or go to town. Every chance encounter between the families was in brooding silence, with Beatty being the first to look the other way.

The Kiplings eventually became so annoyed with Beatty's insistence that he had the legal right to oppose the formal gardens, that they claimed he owed back rent for using the meadows for hay during the past three years. Hearing this, Beatty stormed angrily up to Naulakha to confront them, but found the house closed to him.

Essential communication between Naulakha and Maplewood was by writing, and some notes from Beatty seethed with anger. While Beatty might be harmless when sober, Rudyard thought him a real danger when drunk. By now, Rudyard felt a constant threat, and there were times when despair about the situation made it impossible for him to write.

Despite the stress, a new phase developed for Kipling when Charles Eliot Norton suggested that recent verses entitled "The Native Born" be sent to the *Times* of London. The poem was about the need for unity among the colonies of the British Empire, and it expressed Kipling's (himself of the "native born") awareness of what it meant for someone of English blood and culture to live in another country.

> They change the skies above them,
> But not their hearts that roam!
> We learned from our wistful mothers
> To call old England "home";
>
> * * *
>
> We've drunk to the Queen—God bless her!
> We've drunk to our mothers' land;
> We've drunk to our English brother
> (And we hope he'll understand).

The *Times* was delighted to have "The Native Born," the first of many Kipling poems on current geo-political issues published prominently in its pages. These works had a strong influence on public opinion, and thus on the policies of the British government. Kipling always refused payment for such verses, which he considered a duty to his people, who so admired him.

It was a welcome distraction from the Balestier feud when Rudyard learned to use a pair of Nordic skis left there by Conan Doyle. Thought to be the first pair of skis in Vermont, they attracted immediate interest and attention, as he told a friend: "There was a sober and godly N.Y. lawyer came up about a month ago . . . and I introduced them to him. Since that date he has been wildly trying to get a pair for himself."

"Snow golf" was also a legacy from Conan Doyle's visit. Rudyard played on the snow-covered slope with "Padre" Day, as he called his friend Rev. C.O. Day. They made holes with tin cans stuck into the snow, and inked the golf balls red to keep track of them. Soon the snow was streaked with red from the balls rolling down the hill. Eventually they permanently painted the balls red. Their longer drives bounced and skidded down the slopes, stopped only by stone walls or trees, and there were times—the golfers claimed—that a drive went more than a mile. When the thaw came, they kept on golfing, tramping about the slush in rubber boots.

Rev. Day said of Kipling: "He was intensely interested in all athletics, though playing more like a poet than an athlete. He would discourse most eloquently about the uses of the 'ski,' of snowshoeing and of golf. His play was good, but his dramatic description immensely better."

Kipling apparently well understood the golfer's frustration, for years later his story "The House Surgeon" included a character who despised "this detestable game." As for Rudyard's sportsmanship, Rev. Day recalled an "intentional miss of a hole one inch away, throwing the victory to me, who was a stroke and five yards behind him."

After playing, they would go inside for tea and talk.

Rudyard's daughter was becoming the true joy of his life. In this time he wrote to Joel Chandler Harris of how much Josephine adored being read to from Harris's world of Brer Rabbit.

"And now there is a small maiden, just over three years old, who only knows enough to call the superb Uncle Remus 'The Bunny Book' and this afternoon I have been unfolding to her the mysteries of the tar-baby. She realizes, acutely, that if you hit a tar-baby you can't get away but for the life of her she can't see why. . . . . And it was only the day before yesterday I was lying on my stomach in front of a fire at school reading Uncle Remus on my own hook. So now my debt to you is two generations deep. May you live to see it four."

With Dr. Conland in attendance, Elsie, "a small girl-baby," was born on February 2, 1896. Again, Kipling had hoped for a son, but he was relieved that the pregnancy ended safely.

A few days later, he sent the finished poem "Hymn Before Action" to the *Times* in London, asking the editors to "keep it up your sleeve until the time comes." He wanted them to hold it until the worsening Anglo-American political developments reached such a stage that it would have the most shock-effect—when the poem would be "damned opposite," as he put it. (Although these verses would never be published by the *Times*, they were printed that March by the *Echo,* a New York publication.)

In this same letter to the *Times*, Kipling went on to say, "It is not my business to estimate the chances of war. If things hold off until I can get over the water as I propose doing this summer, I shall be a blooming volunteer private again and then I can open my mouth and make other chaps join. . . . Lord! Lord! what a commentary on civilization!"

Kipling felt the situation between America and Britain rumbling to a climax, and now that the baby had been born, he was resolved to depart with the family later that year. He was still busy with daily chores and responsibilities around Naulakha, and when the snow drifted he went on a road-breaking task with John Bliss and the oxen. Before going out, he took a photograph of Bliss standing in bright sunshine against the barn. (Rudyard later autographed the back of the picture.) He also took an enjoyable day off from writing to watch the building of Naulakha's new gate posts.

More than ever, Rudyard was busy with his story about the cod-fishing fleet. It was to be called *Captains Courageous,* the same title he used for the essay about the Northwest. It was taken from a favorite old ballad, "Mary Ambree." According to Carrington, no other novel absorbed Kipling so completely, and he went several times to Boston Harbor with Conland to meet fishermen. Later, they went to the harbor at Gloucester, Massachusetts, closely questioning the men on the boats and working beside them at the fishing lines. Kipling also learned about the solemn annual memorial service for fishermen lost at sea.

Kipling was powerfully moved by the lives of these folk, and he labored to depict them authentically. *Captains Courageous* is the almost plotless story of a railroad tycoon's spoiled son, who falls overboard from a luxury liner and is rescued by an outbound fishing boat. Since the fishermen cannot turn back to harbor until their boat is full of fish, the boy must stay and work with them for months. Thanks to the honest strength and discipline of the fishermen, he learns to become a man before he rejoins his wealthy family.

McClure's Magazine offered $10,000 for the serial rights.

On March 6th, an editor of the New York *Sunday World* asked Rudyard to write a thousand words at the astounding rate of one dollar per word, on the subject "America could never conquer England." Kipling did not accept. On the same day, word came that Beatty had petitioned for bankruptcy.

Carrie was crushed to hear about her brother, though she had long anticipated it might happen. Soon afterwards, she and Rudyard made a confidential written offer through close friends of Beatty's to help him pay his debts, but under specific conditions. First, Beatty had to leave Maplewood and get employment. Second, the Kiplings would buy Maplewood from him at a reasonable profit—the funds presumably intended to pay Beatty's creditors and get him out of bankruptcy; the Kiplings would sell the farm back when Beatty was solvent again. Third, the Kiplings would take care of Marjorie in the meantime and raise her until Beatty was sober and able to meet his family responsibilities himself.

Beatty refused the offer. Both he and Mai were furious about the Kiplings implying they could give Marjorie a better home.

Carrie was unbearably distraught, especially when the trouble spilled over onto her relationship with her grandmother. By now, old Madam Balestier was upset that Carrie and Rudyard had been pushing Beatty so hard to reform himself. Locals gossiped about how Rudyard was no longer going to Madam Balestier's to visit and read his verses, and Carrie seemed not to stop there with the children as she used to do.

Rudyard tried to escape by throwing himself into work on the New England cod-fishing novel. He had done considerable first-hand research, and the setting intrigued and fascinated him, but he was not yet pleased with its development.

He wrote to a friend, "There ain't two cents worth of plot in the blessed novel—it's all business—cod-fishing on the banks; and no love at all. . . . It's in the nature of a sketch for better work: and I've crept out of possible holes by labeling it a boy's story."

Still, Kipling enjoyed writing this novel, just as he was happy discussing the background of the story with Conland, to whom Rudyard would dedicate the American edition of the book. Much of their talk was in the genial comfort of the Brooks House Hotel bar, with "Colonel" Francis Goodhue II holding court. (The "Colonel" was not a retired regular army officer, but had earned his title after serving on the staff of Gov. Holbrook, Kipling's friend.)

Rudyard noticed that Goodhue wanted to pry into the quarrel with Beatty, and to inquire about Beatty's financial affairs. One day in mid-March, Goodhue said, "People in town think you have been holding Beatty up by the slack of his breeches."

Kipling did not deny the implication, though he did not normally talk about his unhappy relationship with Beatty. A few close friends, such as John Bliss and Conland, knew the family trouble and its history. On this occasion, Kipling conceded to Goodhue that he had indeed supported Beatty up until a year back. As far as Kipling was concerned, this was an open secret anyway, and everyone in town knew about it. Goodhue then implied that creditors in town expected Rudyard to do something to alleviate Beatty's financial problems. Rudyard had no simple reply to that.

To get away from it all, the Kiplings vacationed from mid-March to early April at the Laurel House in Lakewood, near the New Jersey shore. Both Rudyard and Carrie were feeling low in health and spirits, but he perked up by taking bicyling lessons. He loved cycling and bought a "wheel," actually a two-wheel "safety" bicycle model, then becoming popular.

At Lakewood, Rudyard met the famous newspaper magnate, Joseph Pulitzer, publisher of the sensational *New York World* ("rummy company but deuced interesting"). He and the family then spent a week in New York, where they met with author Stephen Crane (*Red Badge of Courage*) and other friends.

At the end of April, they returned to Naulakha, rested. The day after they came back, there arrived a furious letter from Beatty demanding that Rudyard retract "slander" he was spreading. Beatty accused Rudyard of publicly saying, "Oh, Beatty is his own worst enemy. I've been obliged to carry him for the last year; to hold him up by the seat of his breeches."

Shaken, Kipling realized the casual conversation with Goodhue in the Brooks House had rebounded nastily, as gossip will. Mai had heard about it and indignantly complained to Beatty, whose pride was compromised in his wife's eyes. As far as Rudyard was concerned, however, there was nothing to retract and he refused Beatty's written demand to do so.

A few days later, Kipling wrote to England, remarking on photographs of a new house built by a friend there.

"It's very pretty . . ." but "you can't sit on your own piazza and cock your legs up on the railing and listen to the frogs hollerin' on a hot night. Piazzas don't grow in my native land which well I knows it."

He said once they were finished "fixing up things for the spring" at Naulakha, they intended to spend a peaceful summer in the States before returning to England for a prolonged stay.

"I don't want another Vermont winter as yet."

With regard to other work, he was considering writing a children's "fairy book" set in New England. (This idea never got off the ground.)

"I'm supposed to be revising a book of verses," he wrote to another English friend, "but I'm chiefly playing in the garden and racing around with the daughter. The other daughter weighs about 17 lbs. and is a quiet judgmatic kid of a healthy build and an unbounded appetite."

He added that there was "a small boom in real estate up our way on account of the P. O. I got out of Grover. Thus does England benefit even her enemies."

On May 1 there came a letter from college students at Yale, who had just created one of the many Kipling Clubs forming all around the world. They invited him to attend their first banquet.

In the midst of the misery with Beatty and the uncertainty about the international political situation, Rudyard was in no emotional condition to accept. He pulled himself together and, as an apology for not appearing, wrote them a humorous poem in the voice of Mulvaney, one of his well-known Irish redcoats:

> *Attend ye lasses av swate Parnasses*
> *An' wipe my burnin' tears away*
> *For I'm declinin' a chanst o' dinin'*
> *Wid the bhoys of Yale on the fourteenth May.*
> * * *
> *They've made a club there an' staked out grub there*
> *Wid plates an' napkins in a joyous row,*
> *An' they'd think it splindid if I attindid*
> *An' so would I—but I cannot go.*
> * * *
> *When you grow oulder an' skin your shoulder*
> *At the World's great wheel in your chosen line,*
> *You'll find your chances, as Time advances,*
> *For takin' a lark are as slim as mine.*

In these same days, Kipling occasionally passed Balestier on the road—once while Beatty was chatting with men working on the highway, and again when he was standing with Fred Waite near the Waite farm. Neither time did they speak. Rudyard still had not retracted anything Beatty had accused him of saying.

On Wednesday, May 6th, Rudyard set off from Naulakha on his bicycle at about half past four. He headed down the hill to the post office at Waite's, carrying a manuscript for a publisher in England as well as a letter to an old friend from school days at Westward Ho!

"We've no fishing here worse luck," he wrote, "but I'd like you to see what sort of diggings I've made for myself up among these Vermont hills. You can break yourself in three pieces on a bicycle if you like. . . . You must come up and we'll talk things all over. . . ."

He cycled out his driveway, with Maplewood on the left, then Beechwood, and turned down the curve through the shady stand of trees called The Pines. He was picking up speed on the bumpy road, avoiding the wagon ruts, when he heard the rumble of a carriage coming fast down the hill behind him.

Startled, Rudyard wobbled on the bicycle. He was approaching the bottom of the hill as Beatty's buckboard with its snorting team closed in. Rudyard lost control, falling with the bike at the right side of the road just as Beatty swerved across his path.

Rudyard struggled to get up, and Beatty pointed his buggy whip at him, bellowing: "See here! I want to speak to you!"

Sucking blood from a cut on his wrist, Kipling turned to face Beatty and answered sharply, "If you have anything to say, you had better say it to the lawyer."

"By Jesus! This is no case for lawyers!"

Beatty was in a rage, shaking all over, waving a hand in the air. His face was blue, the veins showing, and Rudyard thought he seemed half crazy.

Beatty shouted, "I want you to understand that if you don't retract the goddamn lies you've told about me . . . I'll knock the goddamn soul out of you!"

Kipling did not reply, but stood there with his wrist to his lips, trying to stop the bleeding.

Trembling with fury, Beatty gesticulated and yelled, "You have to retract those goddamned lies within a week . . ." and he went on at Rudyard, who said nothing until Beatty finally threatened to "blow out your goddamned brains!"

Rudyard stiffened. "Let us get this straight. You say if I don't do certain things, you will kill me?"

"By Jesus, I will! I'll give you a week, and if you don't do it, I will kill you!"

Kipling replied, "Remember, you will have only yourself to blame for the consequences."

"Do you dare to threaten me, you little bastard?" Beatty boiled over, calling Rudyard a thief, a coward, and a liar. Then he lashed his ponies on down the hill, turned the buckboard around at the fork of the road, and charged back past Rudyard. Neither man spoke again, and Beatty barreled around the corner, out of sight.

Shaken, Rudyard began to push the bicycle back home. There came another rumble of a carriage from up the road, but this time it was the anxious Matthew Howard, who sprang down to help Rudyard and brought him safely to Naulakha.

Rudyard and Carrie were at a loss for what to do. Rudyard believed Beatty, in a drunken rage, might try to kill him. Nevertheless, Kipling resolved not to retract anything, especially not under a threat.

Meanwhile, Beatty had driven to a friend's house, where he calmed down and said he regretted what had just happened.

Therefore, from job to job I've moved along.
Pay couldn't 'old me when my time was done,
For something in my 'ead upset it all,
Till I 'ad dropped whatever 'twas for good,
An' out at sea, be'eld the dock-lights die,
An' met my mate—the wind that tramps the world!

Sestina of the Tramp-royal, 1896

Chapter 15

Bombay and Brattleboro

It could not have been more of a mistake, but the Kiplings made a decision that caused them unforeseen anguish and heartache: on Thursday, the morning after the ugly incident in The Pines, Rudyard went to the sheriff's office in Brattleboro and laid charges against Beatty.

Apparently, the Kiplings had some notion that the outcome would be a no-nonsense private encounter between Beatty and the sheriff, followed by a stern warning from the sheriff to cease and desist from harassing Rudyard. They had no intention to have Beatty jailed, but they set the gears of justice in motion, and matters soon were out of their hands.

On Saturday, two days later, Beatty was shopping in Brattleboro with Mai and Marjorie when Deputy Sheriff Starkey placed him under arrest, charged with assaulting Kipling with "force of arms," calling him "opprobrious and indecent names" and "threatening to kill."

"These were 'the consequences' to which Kipling had referred darkly," wrote Beatty's friend, Frederic Van de Water. "This was a law-revering Britisher's reprisal. It is possible that he hoped merely to frighten his brother-in-law into contrition. It was, as Kipling shortly learned, dangerous to try to frighten Beatty."

That same day, Beatty was brought to the town hall for a hearing before William S. Newton, the seventy-three-year-old justice of the peace. Rudyard appeared to present his complaint, which was sworn out by state's attorney C.C. Fitts. Local attorney George B. Hitt appeared as counsel for Beatty. Formal statements were taken, and Beatty admitted his violent language but denied threatening Rudyard with anything worse than a beating.

Kipling's lawyers, Edgar W. Stoddard and Kittredge Haskins, requested the hearing be continued on Tuesday, May 12th. The justice granted the request and declared Beatty released on bail. Beatty dismayed Rudyard by saying he had no way to pay bail, which meant he would have to go to jail until the hearing.

The anxious Rudyard stepped forward, his checkbook out, and offered to pay the bail. Beatty snorted refusal. Justice Newton warned he would be locked up until Tuesday if he did not pay bail. Beatty accepted that. Suddenly it became plain to Rudyard that the sordid affair was building up a head of steam. To the outside world, Beatty would look like the persecuted and impoverished American brother-in-law of a vindictive, wealthy Britisher. Preferring jail over letting Rudyard pay his bond, Beatty asked the court for a stay of one hour so he could first bring Mai and Marjorie home.

Exasperated, Justice Newton resolved matters by releasing Beatty on his own recognizance until the Tuesday hearing.

Carrie wrote in her diary that this was the most "wretched and unhappy day" of her life.

By now the local newspapers knew all about it, and that meant the regional and national papers soon would lap it up. Next, the story would flash around the world to newspapers in countries wherever Rudyard Kipling had a following—which was the entire English-speaking world, India, and much of western Europe.

That afternoon there came an offer to Kipling's attorneys from George Hitt, Beatty's counsel, to settle the entire matter, with a full apology to Rudyard. Before this could be put into effect, however, Hitt was called out of town, and by the time he got back the papers had been served by Fitts, the state's attorney for Windham County.

It all might still have blown over, but Beatty soon realized he had an opportunity for both revenge and profit, and he withdrew any offer of apology. There are those who said he telephoned the newspapers about the case.

The Sunday papers from Brattleboro to Washington were gleefully full of the affair. Anti-Kipling editors and reporters all over the country wanted to take a shot at him.

Reporters descended on the town, and Beatty gave interviews—how much he was paid for his side of the story is unknown, but he reveled in the scandal, while Rudyard was shuddering with anger and disgust up at Naulakha. Beatty even went to the train station in his buckboard, picked up loads of reporters, and drove them to Naulakha. Having right-of-way over the Kipling property, he steered his jam-packed buckboard close to the house, pointing and joking with the raucous reporters, sharing drink and loud laughter as they crossed Naulakha's meadow. There was nothing the Kiplings could do about it.

Back at Maplewood, the reporters got Beatty's side of the feud. They were charmed by pretty Mai and plied with whiskey and hard cider. Sweet revenge for the Balestiers, this was turning into a horror that four years ago Kipling could never have imagined would destroy his happy life in Vermont.

On Monday, May 11th, the big-city newspapers were running even longer accounts of the feud, including the history of Wolcott Balestier, his collaboration with Kipling on *The Naulahka*, and how, after the death of Wolcott, Rudyard had married Carrie.

The distraught Balestier family tried to get Beatty to listen to reason and keep the scandal from boiling over. A favorite uncle living locally came to get him to apologize, saying, "Beatty, you can't go on with this! You mustn't. Think of your family."

"Go on with it? What the hell can I do? Goddamn it, who's arrested, anyway?"

Reporters representing newspapers and syndicates around the world were arriving with every train. By the hearing on Tuesday morning, May 12th, more than forty of them crowded with the public into the justice of the peace offices on the ground floor of the town hall.

Justice Newton, a native of nearby Marlboro, moved the hearing to the second floor, in the former town meeting hall, now remodeled and used for lectures and cultural and social affairs. The spacious room was called "Festival Hall."

The hearing had a circus atmosphere, with the eager public crammed into the three galleries along the sides and back of the hall. The press—including newspaper artists with sketch pads and pencils—filled every available space up in front. The judge and witness chair were on a raised stage at one end of the room.

Many spectators were hoping to see Kipling cut down a peg, if not thoroughly embarrassed. After all these years of suffering the anti-American and anti-journalist darts of the haughty Rudyard Kipling, the reporters relished the Englishman's moment of supreme embarrassment. Locals, who wondered just who this reclusive character really was, were delighted by the notoriety and spectacle of the case.

Seated beside attorney Hitt at the defendant's table, a beaming Beatty enjoyed the noisy chaos as Rudyard, bent and nervous, took the stand. Dressed in a jacket and collar with tie, Rudyard nervously twisted a soft hat in his hands. As the plaintiff and the state's only witness, he was questioned by C.C. Fitts, a fellow of about twenty-five.

When starting his career, Fitts had "read law" as a junior partner in the local office that included George Hitt, the defense attorney. Fitts was looked upon as an up-and-coming young lawyer of promise, and the publicity surrounding the Kipling-Balestier affair would certainly put him in the spotlight.

Beatty's attorney, George Hitt, was in his early thirties. A former state's attorney for Windham County, Hitt was considered "a hard man to down," according to local newspapers. He looked forward to elective office in state government

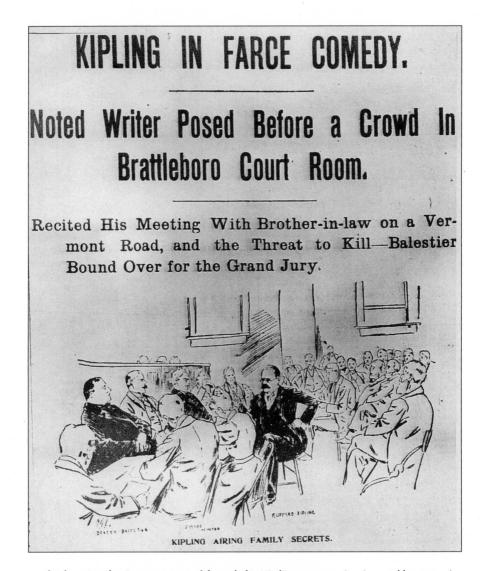

At the hearing for Beatty (second from left), Kipling, center, is pictured by an artist for the *Boston Daily Globe*, morning edition, May 13, 1896, which described the trial as a "farce comedy" with Kipling "airing family secrets."

and, like C.C. Fitts, could see this sensational case as a stepping-stone to fame. Kipling's attorneys, Haskins and Stoddard, were the most respected and experienced firm in Brattleboro.

The brief opening questions by Fitts intended to establish Kipling's version of the incident in The Pines. When asked to relate Beatty's threats, Rudyard at first replied, "Must I use his exact language?"

He did and quoted Beatty's tirade in full, saying Beatty "seemed not in his right senses; crazy. That was my own idea; my impression."

At the end of this first direct examination, he was asked by Fitts, "You may state whether you are, or are not, afraid of him."

Kipling replied, "I honestly think he would kill me if he lost his head again."

Defense attorney Hitt's much longer examination pressed home the fact that Beatty no longer owed Kipling any money. Proceeding through Kipling's hiring of Beatty to manage the Naulakha construction, to the regular work such as hauling goods and hiring workmen for the estate, Hitt established that Beatty Balestier's account with the Kiplings had been paid in full—save for the disputed rent of the hayfield where Carrie wanted to develop a formal garden.

Then Hitt began to thrust: "Isn't it true, Mr. Kipling, that before you went away you told to various persons that Mr. Balestier was largely indebted to you; that you had assisted him—and that your wife had—to large sums of money which he was owing and that he was a sort of pensioner on your bounty."

"Oh, no, not that," Rudyard replied. "I said I had helped him. I was asked the question; several people spoke to me about him. One man said, 'People in town think you have been holding Beatty up by the slack of his breeches.'"

Hitt responded, "You conveyed the idea that you had, didn't you?"

"I might have."

Kipling then insisted he did not generally speak about his relationship with Beatty, but that "the report was in the town before I said anything about it."

Hitt wanted Kipling to admit that he had willfully conveyed a false impression about Beatty to Goodhue at the Brooks House Hotel. Kipling replied that for three years, up until a year ago, he had helped Beatty and tried to maintain a pleasant relationship.

Hitt: "Has that been your mission in America?"

Kipling: "I have done the best I could; I came here for that purpose—to help the boy if I could." He conceded that this had been his main object in coming to the States.

Hitt smiled and said, "Incidentally, you have written some, I suppose?"

Kipling also smiled. "Incidentally, I have written some."

All the while, Rudyard fidgeted uncomfortably in the chair, crossing and uncrossing his legs, crushing and then smoothing out the hat, sometimes dropping it and picking it up. In general, though, he maintained his composure.

Hitt's interrogation was meant to cast doubt on Rudyard's assertion that he had originally come to Vermont to help Beatty. The lawyer referred to the year-long silence between the two households, characterized Kipling's statements about "carrying" Beatty as utterly false, then challenged whether Kipling genuinely wanted to help his brother-in-law.

Hitt laid out the scenario of Beatty trying in vain to speak to Kipling when they met in The Pines, resulting in Beatty's angry demand that they talk. Hitt got Kipling to repeat his reply to Beatty's demand: "If you have anything to say, say it to the lawyer."

Hitt then said, "Was that a furtherance of your purpose which you say you had to have to keep your relations pleasant?"

Kipling: "That was a year ago; I have been nearly crazy ever since."

Throughout the close questioning, Rudyard was firm though not defiant, tense and restless, but not timid. He was on the stand all morning, then again after recess into the afternoon session. It was grueling, but he gave as well as he took.

When Hitt asked whether Kipling feared being shot by Beatty, the answer was, "I have an objection to it."

Hitt frequently assumed the sardonic attitude of the sage country-lawyer, and got some laughs from the gallery—such as when Kipling conceded he had only seen Beatty with a firearm when out hunting, and Hitt rhetorically asked whether Beatty was "gunning for game and not for Kiplings?"

Rudyard's parrying won him grudging admiration from the gallery. When at one point Hitt began to object to question after question by the state's attorney, being overruled by the judge each time, Kipling eventually asked the court, "Er—er—to what question am I answering now?"

When the question was repeated, Kipling looked at the defense counsel and asked, "Have you any objection beforehand, Mr. Hitt?"

Hitt drew himself up and glared in silence.

The *Windham County Reformer* reported: "Mr. Kipling's appearance on the stand was one to reveal the qualities that so attract people that come into close relationship with him, while merely superficial acquaintance is apt to repel. There were not only flashes and sparkles of brightness from that great mine of genius of his, but there were glimpses of the depth and tenderness of feeling that contribute to his power."

When questioned by the state's attorney, Rudyard said the "row began" between him and Beatty when a man was hired to work for Naulakha but was actually employed by Beatty. Rudyard also testified that there were periodic advances of cash to Beatty, who subsequently worked them off, although not always to complete satisfaction. At one point Kipling flatly said he had been supporting Beatty, and his brother-in-law released a loud laugh of derision. Kipling refused to take back what he had said about Beatty: "I wouldn't retract a word under fear of death from any living man."

After the questioning, Rudyard stepped down from the witness chair, with a relieved sigh, fanning himself with his hat as he left the stage. There followed the summary by the attorneys.

When the hearing was finished, Justice Newton promptly announced that Beatty should be held for trial under the charges. The court's next session would begin in September, and in the meantime Beatty could be free on bond. The state's attorney asked for bail of $400 to guarantee Beatty's appearance at county court, and $400 more as a bond for him to keep the peace. Justice Newton surprised everyone by raising the amounts to $500 in each instance.

Kipling had won nothing, for Beatty was gloating more than ever. The impending trial that fall would further expose Rudyard to ridicule and embarrassment. Beatty proceeded to sell his story to the press, while Rudyard let it be known to local friends that he intended soon to leave Vermont.

That evening, Conland, Childs, and Day came to the house to express their sympathy and friendship and the goodwill of many others in Brattleboro. Rudyard appreciated their concern, but was utterly exhausted and weakened, almost ill. In the week after the hearing, Carrie wrote in her diary, "These are dark days for us. Rud is dull, listless and weary." And: "Rud a total wreck. Sleeps all the time, dull, listless and dreary." "Rud very miserable and I most anxious."

From then on, Rudyard carried a gun in his pocket whenever he wandered on the Naulakha hillside. Usually, he was accompanied by Matthew Howard or a friend as further protection against whatever Beatty might do next—especially a drunken Beatty.

The newspapers had their juicy and ludicrously scandalous story about the most famous author in the world. At least one, the *Brattleboro Reformer*, added to the mockery a parody of Kipling's popular redcoat verses, "Danny Deever."

> *"What makes the Kipling breathe so hard?" said the copper ready-made.*
> *"He's mighty scart, he's mighty scart," the First Selectman said.*
> *"What makes his wife look down so glum?" said the copper ready-made.*
> *"It's family pride, it's family pride," the First Selectman said.*

When Rudyard wrote to her on May 14th, Carrie's mother, Anna Balestier, despaired of what to do with Beatty, and answered him the next day:

Thank you for writing, but I am in no wise competent to formulate any ideas as to the future concerning Beatty. . . . Whatever Beatty has done or may do, I must ever continue to keep an affectionate interest in him, being his mother, with the continual hope that it may have some spark of influence, however faint. . . . He is his own worst enemy and always has been, but he has some good impulses, if he would allow them to come to the surface. He has always been an enigma to me which has increased with time. . . .
Your loving Mother

With the international embarrassment, there came an outpouring of sympathy from friends and relations over the Balestier circus. Rudyard's relations with some newspapers were excellent, and the *New York Journal* asked whether he would consider covering the upcoming Republican convention in St. Louis for them. In reply to the editor, declining the offer, Rudyard wrote, "I don't know enough of politics in this land to make the inner meaning of things clear to me."

He added, "As to 'the nightmare,' it is behind me, and I find myself slowly recovering. Do you know 'apo-morphine?' It's a drug, a subcutaneous injection of which makes you heave up your immortal soul. I feel as though about a gallon and a half has been injected into *my* soul but that too will pass away."

Grateful for the kindness of his Brattleboro friends, Rudyard wrote to Gov. Holbrook on May 18th: "I am just in receipt of your very kind letter: and if anything could make amends for such an atrocious affair as last Tuesday's it would be such an expression of sympathy and friendship as you have written.—I am going away tomorrow for a little trip and hope when I come back to feel less sore about the matter."

That month, Rudyard and Dr. Conland went back to Boston Harbor and Gloucester, where they spent enjoyable hours with the cod fishermen, "assisted hospitable tug-masters to help haul three- and four-stick schooners of Pocahontas coal all round the harbor," and watched a derelict hulk suddenly sink at her moorings. Kipling "had sight of the first sickening uprush and vomit of iridescent coal-dusted water into the hold of a ship."

With regard to *Captains Courageous,* Kipling said in his autobiography that his part was the writing, and Conland's "the details. This book took us (he rejoicing to escape from the dread respectability of our little town) to the shore-front, and the old T-wharf of Boston Harbour, and to queer meals in sailors' eating-houses, where he renewed his youth among ex-shipmates or their kin."

He said, "We boarded every craft that looked as if she might be useful, and we delighted ourselves to the limit of delight." One of his souvenirs was "a battered boat-compass, still a treasure with me."

Rudyard returned to Naulahka on May 23rd, and Carrie recorded in her diary that he was in much better spirits, but it was not enough to restore the "nerve and strength which was frittered away in so unworthy a cause." Later that spring, he continued his recuperation on a two-week fishing trip to Quebec's Gaspé region in company with his friend from Long Island, Lockwood de Forest.

In this time, he wrote a ballad entitled "The Feet of the Young Men," about the pleasures of "going with our rods and reels and traces" fishing on "the bar of sun-warmed shingle where a man may bask and dream. . . ."

> *He must go—go—go away from here!*
> *On the other side the world he's overdue.*
> *'Send your road is clear before you when the old*
> *Spring-fret comes o'er you,*
> *And the Red Gods call for you!*

On his return from Canada, Rudyard still gave no outward impression that he meant to leave Naulakha for good, although it was known he meant to be away for some time.

In early June, he wrote to American author William Dean Howells about his future, saying, "I don't think of quitting the land permanently. It is hard to go from where one has raised one's kids, and built a wall and digged a well and planted a tree." Now that the Kiplings were leaving Brattleboro, the case against Beatty would not come to trial.

One of Rudyard's last letters written from Naulakha was to Frank N. Doubleday of Scribners, concerning production details for the forthcoming eleven-volume *Outward Bound* edition of his collected works. He said his father was designing "some sort of conventional little totem" to decorate the edition beside the usual elephant's head with a lotus in the trunk (also originally designed by Lockwood). Added to the elephant's head would be a swastika, the ancient symbol of prosperity and good fortune. An equilateral cross with arms bent at right angles, it is commonly used by Hindus to mark the opening pages of account books and is placed on doorways. (Decades later the swastika would become the symbol of Germany's fascist Nazi party, and when this happened, Kipling stopped using it on his books.)

In mid-July, wrote Carrington, Rudyard "sat down and completed, in a few hours, a composition of one of the most rigorous of all verse-forms. He called it 'Sestina of the Tramp-royal.'"

> *Speakin' in general, I 'ave tried 'em all—*
> *The 'appy roads that take you o'er the world.*
> *Speakin' in general I 'ave found them good*
> *For such as cannot use one bed too long,*
> *But must get 'ence, the same as I 'ave done,*
> *An' go observin' matters till they die.*
>
> * * *
>
> *Therefore, from job to job I've moved along.*
> *Pay couldn't 'old me when my time was done,*
> *For something in my 'ead upset it all,*
> *Till I 'ad dropped whatever 'twas for good,*
> *An' out at sea, be'eld the dock-lights die,*
> *An' met my mate—the wind that tramps the world!*
>
> * * *
>
> *Gawd bless this world! Whatever she 'ath done—*
> *Excep' when awful long—I've found it good.*
> *So write, before I die, "'E liked it all."*

August 29, 1896, was the last day at beloved Naulakha.

The Kiplings arranged to leave the Matthew Howard family in charge of the house, and John Bliss prepared to drive the family to the train station.

Molly Cabot was visiting on that sad day, and she found Carrie busy with final details of the packing. Around Naulakha, the meadows were golden green with the blooming goldenrod Carrie loved so much.

Molly found Rudyard pacing the terrace, in sight of Mount Monadnock. He was pensive, and after a moment spoke softly to her.

"There are only two places in the world where I want to live—Bombay and Brattleboro. And I can't live at either."

James Conland was the only other one to see them off at the station, and he slipped away without saying a final goodbye.

'For far—oh, very far behind,
So far she cannot call to him,
Comes Tegumai alone to find
The daughter that was all to him.'

Merrow Down, 1902

Chapter 16

Departure and Loss

Rudyard and Carrie went with the children to their friends the Catlins in Morristown, New Jersey, to wait until the ship sailed for England.

In a letter from Morristown to William James at Harvard, Kipling said "the curse" of America is "sheer, hopeless, well-ordered boredom; and that is going some day to [be the] curse of the world. The other races are scuffling for their three meals a day. America's got 'em and now she doesn't know what she wants but is dimly realizing that extension lectures, hardwood floors, natural gas and trolley-cars don't fill the bill."

On September 1, 1896, they sailed for England from Hoboken, New Jersey, on the North German liner S.S. *Lahn*. They had arranged to rent an isolated house by the sea at Torquay, on the Devonshire coast. The setting was beautiful, many of the neighbors wealthy, and the site was called "The Riviera of England."

Unlike cool Vermont, the autumn weather on the southern English coast was mild, almost sultry. The Kiplings had all the privacy needed to recover from their summer's ordeal, but this was not Naulakha.

Rudyard wrote to John Hay, "The town is smug British—so that I want to dance naked through it with a pink feather in my stern—but the coast and cliffs and sea are lovely. If *only* we had a little sun! I am not grasping, but Vermont has rather unfitted me for a succession of mildewed days with blobs of yellow wash on the ground, that they trustfully call sunlight."

When winter approached, he wrote to William Hallett Phillips, "I am damp and cold: and my tobacco is like ox-dung newly dropped and I wrap my belly in furs and I swear until I have no more words left."

To Charles Eliot Norton, he said, ". . . I have been studying my fellow countrymen from outside. Those four years in America will be blessed unto me for all my life. . . . Carrie takes well to our infernal climate but Josephine has a cold. . . . I long sometimes for a clear October morning with a touch of frost."

By Carrie's birthday, December 31, 1896, Kipling was looking back wistfully on his Vermont time, saying Josephine was truly an American child. "We had a very nice American Christmas," he told Norton, adding "I don't think we can stay out a whole year longer without coming over to have a look at things. It's an uncivilized land (I still maintain it) but how the deuce has it wound itself around my heartstrings in the way it has? C and I sit over our inadequate English fire and grow–homesick."

The Kiplings soon moved to another house, this one in Rottingdean, on the Sussex coast. There they were surrounded by his family and old friends, who lived nearby. They doted on their children, and Rudyard expressed his fatherly distractions in a *Just So Stories* poem about answering Josephine's unending questions:

> *I keep six honest serving men*
> *(They taught me all I knew);*
> *Their names are What and Why and When*
> *And How and Where and Who.*

Kipling lets them rest sometimes, but

> *Different folk have different views;*
> *I know a person small—*
> *She keeps ten million serving-men*
> *Who get no rest at all!*

Internationally, the Anglo-American troubles were in the process of being defused by arbitrators. Cleveland had lost the 1896 presidential election in spite of his twisting the British lion's tail, and a new American administration under William McKinley came in. Relations between the two countries improved, moving toward the eventual creation of the 20th-century alliance against Germany and her allies. Gradually, the wound of the American crisis healed.

Rudyard stayed in touch with American friends, especially with Conland, Doubleday (who soon founded his own publishing company with Rudyard as his premier author), Teddy Roosevelt, and Norton. He dedicated the Gaspé fishing journey's verses, "The Feet of the Young Men," to his Washington friend, William Hallett Phillips, who in 1897 drowned in a boating accident.

That year was the Diamond Jubilee celebration of Queen Victoria's reign, and many a poetic tribute was penned in commemoration. As the months passed, however, nothing was written about the Jubilee by Rudyard Kipling, the real national poet. The British public waited expectantly, but by Jubilee Day, June 22nd, as the whole empire paraded and glittered and toasted itself, Kipling had not produced a "ceremonial ode."

On July 16th, after spending two weeks as the navy's guest of honor on maneuvers in the English Channel, Rudyard was visited in his Rottingdean study by Sallie Norton, daughter of his dear American friend, Charles Eliot Norton. Kipling was sorting and discarding work, and Sallie asked permission to look at a sheet he had thrown into the waste paper basket. It was entitled "After."

Sallie was moved by the verses and said it ought to be published. Carrie and one of Kipling's favorite aunts, also there on a visit, agreed, and he began to revise it. Sallie suggested the repetition of the last couplet of the first stanza:

> *Lord God of Hosts be with us yet,*
> *Lest we forget—lest we forget!*

The poem, reading much like a hymn, was sent to the *Times* office and appeared in the paper the next day, under Kipling's new title, "Recessional."

Carrington wrote: "Again Kipling astonished the nation by revealing its heartfelt but unrealized emotion. Humility not pride, awe not arrogance, a sense of transience not a sense of permanence were to be the keynotes of the imperial festival."

> *God of our fathers, known of old,*
> *Lord of our far-flung battle line,*
> *Beneath whose awful Hand we hold*
> *Dominion over palm and pine—*
> *Lord God of Hosts, be with us yet,*
> *Lest we forget—lest we forget!*

> *The tumult and the shouting dies;*
> *The Captains and the Kings depart:*
> *Still stands Thine ancient sacrifice,*
> *An humble and a contrite heart.*
> *Lord God of Hosts, be with us yet,*
> *Lest we forget—lest we forget!*

Greater public praise than ever before poured in, from pacifists and imperialists alike. Kipling's star was never brighter, and to this glory was added the birth of a son, John, on August 17th.

Carrie with John, Elsie, and Josephine in 1898.

Still, there was a longing for his Vermont home. Rudyard wrote to Norton that month in thanks for a letter, saying they were "cheered immensely" to hear from him, but "Sallie at Rottingdean, you at Ashfield and we away from Naulakha with bits of the downs for Monadnock mixed things up. It would have been all right if you had come in from the garden with Taffy."

In January, 1898, the Kiplings went to Cape Town, South Africa, to escape the bleak chill of English winter.

In South Africa Rudyard became fast friends with Cecil Rhodes, the dominant political force in the British African colonies. A self-made millionaire in diamond mines, Rhodes built a cottage exclusively for the Kiplings, who would make winter journeys to South Africa for years to come.

The Day's Work was published in 1898, containing the stories written in Vermont. For the fourth time, Rudyard again turned to the long novel, *Kim,* which had eluded him in his Naulakha period. By now, he was considered the most important and influential British writer of the day, although many of the opinions he expressed in verse and prose seemed increasingly conservative.

Yet, other things he said showed that, despite the distorted interpretations of critics, he was not to be pegged to a single, inflexible political position. His point of view is witnessed by a letter written from Naulakha late in 1895 to the American Board of Foreign Missions of the Presbyterian Church. The missionary board had apparently asked for his opinion on the subject of missions and contemporary practices with regard to converting and teaching indigenous peoples.

Kipling replied: "It is my fortune to have been born and to a large extent brought up among those whom white men call 'heathen' and while I recognize the paramount duty of every white man to follow the teachings of his creed and conscience . . . it seems to me cruel that white men, whose governments are armed with the most murderous weapons known to science, should amaze and confound their fellow creatures with a doctrine of salvation imperfectly understood by themselves and a code of ethics foreign to the climate and instincts of those races whose most cherished customs they outrage and whose gods they insult."

With these words Kipling expressed a sentiment that he said "has been very near to my heart." The label of bigoted imperialist that was pinned on him in later years was largely a result of (sometimes intentional) misinterpretation of his work, including "The White Man's Burden," first published in February, 1899.

> *Take up the White Man's burden—*
> *The savage wars of peace—*
> *Fill full the mouth of Famine*
> *And bid the sickness cease;*
> *And when your goal is nearest*
> *The end for others sought,*
> *Watch Sloth and heathen Folly*
> *Bring all your hope to nought.*

This poem often has been interpreted exactly opposite of Kipling's actual meaning. He does not encourage civilized whites to dominate weaker cultures, but instead describes the toiling idealists, administrators, engineers, doctors, nurses, and civil servants, who set out to aid the needy. He warns them to be prepared to suffer defeat and sorrow for their altruistic pains.

One alternative meaning of the term "white man" as commonly used then was to indicate someone who was "white" or "pure" of heart, with honest motives in keeping with the humanistic standards of the day. As biographer Carrington put it, the work of colonial civil servants was "a task to be done without material reward, without thanks, without even a confident hope of success."

Certainly the wealth and power of empire was of no material benefit to thousands of white civil servants carrying the burden of their ideals. For the most part, they did what they did out of a sense of responsibility, not with the intent to subjugate native peoples.

> *Take up the White Man's burden—*
> *No tawdry rule of kings,*
> *But toil of serf and sweeper—*
> *The tale of common things.*
> *The ports ye shall not enter,*
> *The roads ye shall not tread,*
> *Go make them with your living,*
> *And mark them with your dead!*

Kipling intended "The White Man's Burden" to speak to the United States, fast rising to international power after defeating Spain in 1898 and taking over a new colonial empire. In a letter to an American friend that summer, Kipling said Americans were finally assuming a place of responsibility among the advanced nations. He went on: "they are equals (which for all their wealth they were not before)" and they "have justified themselves as White Men." He added that now "they understand things" and "each year of administering alien races . . . will educate, stiffen and cleanse" Americans.

The States must begin to "help races who have never conceived the western notion of liberty." Referring to the American "tribe," Kipling said he had "come pretty close to understanding that section of the Tribe among whom I built my house and raised a couple of babies. . . ."

He encouraged America to take over the Philippines and administer it, despite the fighting and bloodshed that inevitably would follow. He predicted he would write something about it all, and closed by welcoming the United States into the group of nations with responsibility for bearing the "white man's burden": "You've come into the Tribe for keeps now, and no one is more pleased than Yours always sincerely, Rudyard Kipling."

When "The White Man's Burden" was published on February 4th in the *Times*, Rudyard and his family were back in America, having arrived in New York City on February 2nd.

The Kiplings came to New York partly to resolve another annoying copyright dispute with an American publisher. Rudyard felt he could best attend to it in person, believing his presence in the States and willingness to go to court would do much to dissuade American publishers from infringing on his rights.

Furthermore, Rudyard and Carrie wanted to go back to Naulakha, perhaps to arrange for disposing of the house, or perhaps to reopen it, as friends in New England hoped. Rudyard's mother, Alice, had tried to change their minds about making an Atlantic crossing in winter, and her worst fears came to pass.

The entire family caught severe colds on the voyage. What was worse, they were kept waiting for two hours at the chill and drafty New York customs house, surrounded by pestering reporters. Rudyard would say nothing to them, and was distracted by the coughing and fevers of his children.

At their suite in Manhattan's Hotel Grenoble on West 56th Street, the children were diagnosed as having whooping cough with complications. Their cases soon grew worse, and Dr. Conland arrived to help attend to them. Also on hand were a number of friends and Dr. Theo Dunham, husband of Carrie's sister, Josephine.

The Manhattan streets were blocked by a heavy snowfall, and scores of reporters swarmed around the hotel, trying to get a glimpse of Rudyard. Then came the distressing news that Beatty had declared himself prepared to charge Rudyard with malicious prosecution, demanding $50,000 compensation.

On February 8th, while Rudyard and Carrie were especially fearful for the girls, Carrie, too, fell ill with fever. Her iron will imparted enough strength to master the sickness, however, and she and Rudyard attended to business, even going to social affairs. The weather relented, and the children improved, although the whole family had persistent coughs.

Plans were made to go to Boston and the Nortons, and the people of Brattleboro speculated that Naulakha would at last be reopened that spring. Vermont friends, said a local newspaper, had hailed the Kiplings' anticipated return "with solemn joy" and planned "dinners of state" in Rudyard's honor.

On February 20th the Kiplings went for a visit to Central Park, and that afternoon Rudyard was the guest of the Century Club. When he came back to the hotel, he was feverish and weary. The next day, he fell seriously ill with pneumonia, suffering from a cough and reddish expectorate. A specialist and a night nurse were brought in, and one lung was diagnosed to be dangerously inflamed.

The lung soon filled, making it hard to breathe, and the second began to do the same. Though at risk of asphyxiation, Rudyard managed to sleep much of this time. The outcome was uncertain, and his lifelong tendency toward fever was a threat. Carrie wrote in her diary that "good friends and helping hands" meant so much just then. "I feel how everyone Rud has ever spoken to has loved him, and is glad and happy to help do for him."

Meanwhile, as the days passed, six-year-old Josephine entered a high fever and was taken from the hotel to the De Forest home on Long Island. Carrie wrote that parting with her daughter was "agony." Conland attended to the child he had brought into the world at Bliss Cottage, and Carrie stayed with the half-conscious Rudyard.

From February 23rd to April 17th, Carrie scarcely wrote in her diary.

Carrington said: "There she was, in an uptown New York hotel, weakened after her own bout of fever, in charge of two children—one aged three years, the other aged eighteen months—both with the whooping-cough, torn with anxiety for her darling elder daughter, her doors besieged by press reporters, her irresponsible brother Beatty threatening her with an action, her husband's affairs deeply involved in legal complications, and her husband fighting for his life—delirious for many days."

Rudyard's crisis was met on the night of February 28th.

He could scarcely breathe, and only the labors of doctors and nurses seemed to keep him alive. The second lung was almost solidified. Carrie wrote to Charles Eliot Norton, "We are making a strong fight and may win or lose any hour."

Then, miraculously, the first lung began to resume its function. Kipling fell into a coma-like sleep. He was still in danger, but there was hope for recovery.

Carrie stood up to all this, with friends and family at her side, but with the ultimate weight and dread on her shoulders. The hotel lobby was jammed with reporters hungry for daily news of Kipling's health. Frank Doubleday stepped in as a rock-solid friend to deal with and inform the reporters, who ran front-page stories about Kipling's illness day after day for a month.

Crowds gathered in silence outside the hotel. Prayers and vigils were led in New York houses of worship. All around the world, there was no more newsworthy event, except that Pope Leo XIII also was gravely ill. Hundreds of letters and telegrams were sent to the hotel. Henry James, who once had doubted the future of the Kipling marriage, wrote, "My Dear Daemonic Indestructible Youth, You are a good one, and your wife is, if possible, a better. . . ."

James wrote his letter on March 6th, the same day Carrie entered in her diary: "Josephine left us at 6:30 this morning."

Rudyard was so weak that the doctors insisted he not yet be told about Josephine's death.

Carrie hurried back from the funeral (Josephine was buried at the cemetery in Fresh Pond, Long Island) and went to see him. Realizing at the last moment she was dressed in black, Carrie threw a scarlet shawl around her shoulders so Rudyard would not notice.

Carrington wrote, "How and when she broke the news to him is their own secret. Months passed before he recovered from his illness; from the shock of his daughter's death he never recovered; nor did Carrie."

It was not until Easter, after a gloomy convalescence, that Rudyard answered the world's expressions of respect and love. In an open letter published in hundreds of newspapers, he acknowledged the "wonderful sympathy, affection, and kindness shown toward me in my recent illness. . ." and being unable to answer all letters in person "must take this means of thanking, as humbly as sincerely, the countless people of goodwill throughout the world, who have put me under a debt I can never hope to repay."

Cared for by the faithful Doubleday, the Kiplings went to Lakewood in mid-April, along with Lockwood Kipling, who had arrived when the crisis was past. A few weeks later, Conland said the lung was healed, but Kipling should never again spend a winter in cold, damp England, lest he suffer a relapse that would be fatal.

Early in May, Kipling was offered an honorary Doctor of Laws degree by McGill University in Montreal. Conferred in absentia on June 16th, this was the first of his academic honors—the only type of formal honor he would ever accept.

From mid-May to early June, the Kiplings stayed with the Catlins in Morristown. Rudyard was forbidden to work for at least six months. He was weak, his drifting thoughts much upon Josephine, but he showed immense self-control and courage.

Perhaps speaking for them both, Carrie wrote in her diary, "I have only scraps of mind left me, and so no memory except of these black weeks just passed."

Reminiscences of New Jersey friends describe Kipling in his baggy trousers and slouch hat, taking walks on the roads around Morristown, sitting and chatting with housewives on their stoops. One writer said, "he seemed to extract more enjoyment out of talking with the plain country folks" than with anyone else. He occasionally went for long carriage drives around Essex County, through the Oranges, Montclair, and Newark. He visited Paterson to see the locomotive works and the silk industry there.

The Kiplings spent early June at Doubleday's home in Cold Spring Harbor, Long Island. In mid-June, Carrie made a secret journey to Brattleboro. The Howard family was living in the carriage house, but Naulakha was silent, the garden overgrown. Drapes brought from India still hung in the house, and in the attic was Rudyard's old writing desk from England, with the inscription carved upon it: "Oft was I weary as I toiled at Thee." The desk would stay at Naulakha, but Carrie gave orders to have the inscription removed.

She hastily arranged for some personal possessions to be shipped back to England, and for some reason left documents and papers in their bank's safe deposit box, including her marriage certificate, scraps of original Kipling manuscript and verse, an old will of Rudyard's, and the copy of the poem "The Long Trail," which Rudyard had dedicated to her.

In this time, Beatty asked Matthew Howard about the coming of the Kiplings, but was told nothing, so he did not trouble Carrie. She stayed at Mrs. Kirkland's boarding house on Main Street, Brattleboro, leaving town after only two days. On June 14, 1899, the Kiplings departed for England.

A few weeks later, Rudyard wrote a letter of gratitude to an old friend, the American Edmonia "Ted" Hill, whom he had so admired—and perhaps loved platonically—when he was a young writer and she was married to a professor in India.

"I don't think it is likely that I shall ever come back to America. My little Maid loved it dearly (she was almost entirely American in her ways of thinking and looking at things) and it was in New York that we lost her. Everybody was more than kind to us and to her but I don't think I could face the look of the city again without her."

The Kiplings never again returned to the United States or Naulakha. Their home in Rottingdean was sadly darkened by the shadows of Josephine's memories. In 1902, Rudyard published the *Just So Stories* he so often had told to Josephine, "Taffy," the "Best Beloved" of her dream-spinner father, Tegumai. The central poem of the book is "Merrow Down," set in southern England's rolling down country in Surrey, where Rudyard and Josephine had often gone for walks.

In these verses, Rudyard first evokes images of ancient Britain, and then:

> *'But long and long before that time*
> *(When bison used to roam on it)*
> *Did Taffy and her Daddy climb*
> *That Down, and had their home on it.*

Now, Taffy and the Tribe of Tegumai are no more, and:

>'On Merrow Down the cuckoos cry—
>   The silence and the sun remain.
>
>'But as the faithful years return
>   And hearts unwounded sing again,
>Comes Taffy dancing through the fern
>   To lead the Surrey spring again.
>
>'Her brows are bound with bracken-fronds,
>   And golden elf-locks fly above;
>Her eyes are bright as diamonds
>   And bluer than the sky above.
>
>'In moccasins and deer-skin cloak,
>   Unfearing, free and fair she flits,
>And lights her little damp-wood smoke
>   To show her Daddy where she flits.
>
>'For far—oh, very far behind,
>   So far she cannot call to him,
>Comes Tegumai alone to find
>   The daughter that was all to him!'

If you can talk with crowds and keep your virtue,
  Or walk with Kings—nor lose the common touch,
If neither foes nor loving friends can hurt you,
  If all men count with you, but none too much;
If you can fill the unforgiving minute
  With sixty seconds' worth of distance run,
Yours is the Earth and everything that's in it,
  And—which is more—you'll be a Man, my son!

If—, 1910

Epilogue

On January 12, 1936, Rudyard Kipling dictated a letter to William H. Evans of Philadelphia. Evans intended to donate a set of Kipling's works to the public library in Townshend, Vermont, the community next to Dummerston and Naulakha, and he had written to Rudyard asking for a message from the author to accompany the gift.

Kipling was 70, Carrie 73. Since June, 1902, their home had been a secluded estate in Sussex, England, called Bateman's. The square, stone manor house, built in the 1600s, had extensive formal gardens that were under Carrie's charge, and along one path was goldenrod, nurtured as a memory of America, where it grew wild.

Over the years, another profound sorrow had come upon the Kiplings when their son, John, had gone missing at the age of seventeen in an early battle of the Great War. Now, Rudyard was often ill with painful intestinal difficulties that the doctors seemed unable to cure. Although daughter Elsie was happily married to George Bambridge, a former soldier in John's regiment, the Irish Guards, there were no Kipling grandchildren to liven up the estate.

Since 1896 there had been no more contact with Beatty Balestier, who once declared to the writer, Van de Water, "He never came back. He never will come while I'm alive." Beatty mostly blamed Carrie for the trouble, saying "it was a family row," and that he and Rudyard would have been good friends otherwise. (Beatty had his own sorrows, Mai and Marjorie both dying young; he was to die in mid-1936, impoverished and sickly, but still a hearty fellow, well liked in Brattleboro.)

With the purchase of Bateman's, the Kiplings had removed from Naulakha all they wanted to keep. The estate was sold in 1903 to Molly Cabot for $8,000, far below cost. Beatty at first had threatened to contest the title, and thus the selling price had been so depressed. James Conland was offered the guns and rods and sporting gear left behind, and John Bliss got Conan Doyle's skis.

Lockwood Kipling used his skill at *bas relief* to create illustrations for his son's novel *Kim,* set in India, where Lockwood once headed an art school.

Molly Cabot never lived at Naulakha, and she in turn sold it in 1922 to her nephew, F. Cabot Holbrook. Now, the house was used only as a summer residence, and it was much the same as when the Kiplings had lived there, even most of their furniture still in place.

After the tragedy of 1899, the Kiplings had returned to North America only twice: in 1907 for a Canadian tour, and again briefly to Canada in 1930. They did not cross the border to the United States. Yet there were many friends and correspondents in the States, such as Evans in Philadelphia to whom Kipling dictated the letter. Evans had reminded Kipling of those snowbound winters in Vermont, when sometimes the only recreation was to read.

In the dictated letter of reply, Kipling said: "As I used to know well, Vermont winters are long (I have been on runners from Thanksgiving to almost April, though I suppose now there isn't a sleigh left in the state) and so I am very sympathetic to your idea of building up the Townshend library. After all, I have an indirect interest in the institution insofar as I wrote the first *Jungle Book* with four feet of snow on the ground almost next to Townshend. With every good wish, Sincerely, —."

Before the letter was typed out by his secretary, Rudyard set off with Carrie to visit Elsie at her home in Hampstead. He intended to sign the letter on his return to Bateman's. The Kiplings stayed at Brown's Hotel in London, where they had spent their first days of marriage. They made plans to vacation soon at Cannes in France, a country where he was much loved and widely read in translation.

Rudyard was as famous as ever, and the most quoted of all contemporary authors. According to Carrington: "Whether liked or disliked, he was the only poet of his day whose verse was known by men and women of all classes, all creeds, all walks of life." There were active Kipling Societies in five countries, and much of his earlier work was still extremely popular, especially *The Jungle Books* and *Just So Stories*, which became an early childhood memory for millions who first heard them read by adults. To those children, the "Best Beloved" was, of course, none other than themselves.

Kipling had been awarded the Nobel Prize for literature in 1907; films had been made of his books; he was wealthy, and was a friend and confidant to royalty and prime ministers. But his power as an important and timely British voice had burned out. His latest writing—essays, short stories, and verse—was more brilliant than ever, delicately subtle and intuitive, but the next work by Kipling was no longer eagerly awaited by a huge, enthusiastic public as it had been at the turn of the century. Rudyard's coined phrases yet gleamed hard and smooth as part of everyday language, though it was forgotten that he had conceived them. "Main

Street"; "White Man's Burden"; ". . . who only England know"; "If you can keep your head when all about you are losing theirs and blaming it on you"; "Law of the Jungle"; "East is East and West is West and never the twain shall meet"; "An' the dawn comes up like thunder"; "For the female of the species is more deadly than the male," and more.

Kim, developed at Naulakha and published in 1900, had been his finest triumph as a novelist. As for *Captains Courageous,* however, it had a mixed reception, especially by critics in the States, who called the tale a misguided depiction of the old, long-gone Gloucester fishing fleet, not the fleet or fishermen of the day.

Kipling's most famous poems—"Recessional," "The Ballad of East and West," "Gunga Din"—stood against time, and "If" was translated into twenty-seven languages, quoted year after year at thousands of graduation ceremonies. But misunderstood, controversial verses such as "The White Man's Burden" had earned lasting hostility from those who considered him a racist, even ending friendships with some of the New England intellectuals he once had known.

His birthday that December, 1935, had been publicly celebrated by admirers around the world, yet Rudyard was regularly condemned by some influential writers as a shameless imperialist. Though unswervingly anti-communist, he was falsely accused of favoring fascism. Rudyard certainly admired stable political order, old-fashioned social values, and strong, honest leaders—he was a staunch political conservative—but he was first of all an independent man, still with two sides to his head, and his ideas belonged to no one.

Year after year, Rudyard had refused all titles from king and state, accepting only honorary literary degrees, and there were many. When Julia Catlin of Morristown, N.J., asked why he refused even the Order of Merit, the highest honor of the British Empire, and more than once declined the king's personal wish that he be knighted, Rudyard said to her, "I prefer to live and die just Rudyard Kipling."

At Brown's Hotel, in the early hours of January 13, 1936, Rudyard had a sudden violent internal hemorrhage and was rushed to Middlesex Hospital. In and out of consciousness, he lay close to death for five days. As in 1899, the entire world watched and waited, reporters and photographers surrounding the hospital.

During this time, his secretary sent the letter of reply to William Evans in Philadelphia, dating it January 13th and saying "Mrs. Kipling thought that, in spite of its lack of signature, you would like to have it."

Thus, a letter about Vermont was perhaps the last thing Rudyard Kipling wrote, for he died just after midnight, January 18, 1936, on his 44th wedding anniversary. His ashes were placed in Westminster Abbey's Poets' Corner.

EPILOGUE

If there be good in that I wrought
Thy Hand compelled it, Master, Thine—
Where I have failed to meet Thy Thought
I know, through Thee, the blame was mine.

The depth and dream of my desire
The bitter paths wherein I stray—
Thou knowest Who hast made the Fire,
Thou knowest Who hast made the Clay.

My New-cut Ashlar, 1890

THE END

Acknowledgments

As with so much of Rudyard Kipling's life and work, the story of his Brattleboro years still affects and moves people today. Some of those people contributed to this book, and in turn have given something back to the memory of Rudyard Kipling, in gratitude for all he gave to us.

Thanks to Tordis Ilg Isselhardt, publisher of Images from the Past, and to Barbara George, publisher of Whetstone Publishing in Brattleboro, Vermont, and to Peter and Victoire Gardner, publishers of The Centinel Company in Hanover, New Hampshire, who all saw the importance of telling the story of Kipling's Vermont period.

Thanks to Sally Andrews, librarian of the Howard C. Rice Library at Marlboro College, Marlboro, Vermont, whose expertise with the library's Kipling collection was essential to understanding the history behind this story. Thanks also to the library's staff, mostly Marlboro students, whose efforts made it possible for the author to delve efficiently into the voluminous Kipling archive over the course of eighteen months' research.

I am also grateful to those who took the time to read and improve the manuscript: John Wallace of Putney, Vermont, who generously shared his extensive knowledge of Kipling's life and times at Naulakha and in southern Vermont; Kipling scholar Thomas Pinney of Claremont, California, who has so expertly collected and annotated volumes of Kipling's letters, offering an intimate view of Kipling's personal thoughts and experiences in these years; David C. Tansey, architectural conservator for Naulakha and The Landmark Trust; and to J. Birjepatil, Kipling scholar and professor at Marlboro College.

I am grateful once again for the editorial abilities of Sarah Novak of Richmond, Massachusetts. Another fine editor, Tyler Resch of North Bennington, Vermont, contributed invaluable comments to improve the manuscript. To these readers go much of the credit for that which is right in this book, and I bear responsibility for the rest.

Thanks to The Landmark Trust USA, owners of Naulakha, for permission to reproduce many of the Kipling photographs that illustrate this book. Also thanks to Carol Barber of The Landmark Trust for her kindness and help in many ways.

Also, thanks, for the use of photographs of the Balestier family, to the Rochester Historical Society.

For assistance and encouragement, thanks to Thomas Ragel, past president of Marlboro College for permitting my research in the Rice papers; to the Brooks Public Library in Brattleboro and the Brattleboro Historical Society; and to Geoffrey Brown, professor at Marlboro whose study of Beatty Balestier inspired him to write a one-man play.

Thanks also to the Brattleboro Museum & Art Center, whose exhibit "A Tale of Bliss and Tragedy," gave a close look at Kipling's life at Naulakha. Thanks to Barbara Krieger, archives assistant at the Dartmouth College Library, Hanover, New Hampshire, for her kind assistance.

The staff members at the Kinderhook Memorial Library, Kinderhook, New York, were essential to my research, as was the staff at the East Greenbush Area Library, East Greenbush, New York. Thanks also to George Engel of Book Creations, Canaan, New York, for generous use of his computers and copier and printers.

And once again, as so often before, I am indebted to the Chatham Public Library, Chatham, New York, for its efforts on my behalf: Cynthia Maguire, director; Wendy Fuller, interim director; Carolyn Brust and Elizabeth Gaupman.

Finally, it should be stressed that the extensive Kipling archive in Marlboro College is composed mainly of the papers of the late Howard C. Rice, whose life's work made him the outstanding expert on the life of Rudyard Kipling in Vermont. It is sincerely hoped that *Rudyard Kipling in Vermont* would have been worthy of Mr. Rice's wholehearted approval.

Bibliography

Unless otherwise noted, all quotations from Kipling's poetry are taken from *Rudyard Kipling's Verse, Inclusive Edition, 1885–1918.*

BOOKS

Beresford, C.G. *Schooldays With Kipling.* New York: G.P. Putnam's Sons, 1936.

Birkenhead, F.W. *Rudyard Kipling.* New York: Random House, 1978.

Cabot, Mary. *Annals of Brattleboro.* Brattleboro: Press of E. L. Hildreth & Co., 1921–22.

Carr, John Dickson. *The Life of Sir Arthur Conan Doyle.* New York: Harper, 1949.

Carrington, Charles E. *The Life of Rudyard Kipling.* Garden City, New York: Doubleday & Co., Inc.

Crane, Charles E. *Pen-drift.* Brattleboro: Stephen Daye Press, 1931.

Dobree, Bonamy. *Rudyard Kipling.* London: Longmans, Green and Co., 1951.

Eliot, T.S. *A Choice of Kipling's Verse.* New York: Faber, 1942.

Emerson, Ralph Waldo. Poetry collection. *Essays and Poems of Emerson.* New York: Harcourt Brace & Company, 1921.

Mason, Philip. *Kipling, The Glass, The Shadow and The Fire.* New York: Harper & Row, 1975.

Paine, Albert B. *Mark Twain: A Biography,* 2 Vols. Philadelphia: Richard West, 1912.

Pinney, Thomas. *Kipling's India: Uncollected Sketches 1884–88.* Basingstoke, Hampshire: MacMillan, 1986.

—. *Rudyard Kipling: Something of Myself and Other Biographical Writings.* New York: Cambridge University Press, 1990.

—. *Rudyard Kipling's Letters.* 2 Vols. Iowa City: University of Iowa Press, 1990.

Seymour-Smith, Martin. *Rudyard Kipling.* New York: St. Martin's Press, 1989.

Stewart, J.I.M. *Rudyard Kipling.* New York: Dodd, Mead & Co., 1966.

Stewart, James McG. *Rudyard Kipling: A Biographical Catalogue.* Toronto: Dalhousie University, 1959.

Twain, Mark. *Autobiography of Mark Twain.* New York: Harper & Row, 1975.

Van de Water, Frederic. *Rudyard Kipling's Vermont Feud.* Rutland: Academy Books, 1936.

Wilson, Angus. *The Strange Ride of Rudyard Kipling.* New York: Viking Press, 1977.

ARTICLES

Day, Rev. C.O. "Rudyard Kipling as Seen in His Vermont Home." *The Congregationalist,* March 16, 1899.

Editors. "Mr. Kipling's Green Mountain Home." *The Critic,* Jan. 21, 1893.

Forbes, Charles S. "Rudyard Kipling in Vermont." *The Vermonter.* Vol. IV, No. 9 (April, 1899).

Gosse, Sir Edmund. "Questions at Issue." Heinemann, 1893.

Hamner-Croughton, Amy. "The Wife of Rudyard Kipling: Caroline Balestier." *The Rochester Historical Society, Vol. VI, 1927.*

Hill, Donald. "Kipling in Vermont." *Nineteenth Century Fiction.* Vol. 7, No. 3 (December, 1952): 153-170.

Hueguenin, Charles A. "Rudyard Kipling and Brattleboro." *Vermont History.* Vol. XXIV, No.1 (January 1956): 39-52.

Milner, Florence. "We Call on Mrs. Kipling at Bateman's." *Boston Evening Transcript,* Jan. 2, 1926.

Parsons, Margaret G. "A Close-up of Kipling." *The Sunday Telegram,* Worcester, Mass., February 23, 1926.

Rice, Howard C. "Kipling's Winters in Vermont." *UpCountry.* Vol. 2, No. 2 (February 1974): 8-9, 14-15, 26.

Rice, Howard C. "Rudyard Kipling's House in Vermont." *Vermont Life.* Vol. VI, No. III (Spring 1952): 34-39.

Rice, Howard C. "Rudyard Kipling in Vermont." *The New England Quarterly.* Vol. IX, No. 3 (September 1936): 363-377.

Shaw, Donald. "Trolley Days in Brattleboro, Vermont." A Connecticut Valley Chapter National Railway Historical Society Publication. (April, 1948).

Stoddard, Charles Warren. "Rudyard Kipling at Naulakha." *National Magazine,* XXII (June, 1905): 259-268.

Tansey, David. "Naulakha: House Tour Guide." Landmark Trust Brochure, 1994.

Taufflieb, J.H.C. "Memories of Rudyard Kipling." *The Kipling Journal,* October & December, 1943.

Wallace, John A. "A Tale of Bliss and Tragedy." Brattleboro Museum Brochure, May 14, 1994.

UNPUBLISHED WORKS

Haffner, Donald. "Naulakha, The House that Rudyard Kipling Built." 1979 Independent Study, Marlboro College, Marlboro, Vt.

Miller, Juliette. "Recollections of Beatty Balestier." 1980. Marlboro College, Marlboro, Vt.

Rice, Howard C. Research Notes and Papers for ms. "Kipling's Vermont Years." Marlboro College, Marlboro, Vt.

Unclaimed Kipling Papers from the Vermont National Bank; Marlboro College, Marlboro, Vt.

WORKS BY RUDYARD KIPLING

—. *A Book of Words.* Garden City: Doubleday, Doran & Company, 1928.

—. *Captains Courageous.* New York: Doubleday & Co., 1920.

—. *From Sea to Sea: Letters of Travel.* New York: Doubleday & McClure Company, 1899.

—. *Day's Work, The.* New York: Doubleday & McClure Company, 1899.

—. *Light that Failed, The.* Garden City: Doubleday, Page & Company, 1925.

— and Wolcott Balestier. *Naulahka, The.* New York: Macmillan and Co., 1895.

—. *Seven Seas, The.* New York: Appleton and Company, 1898.

—. *Something of Myself.* Garden City: Doubleday, Doran & Company, 1937.

—. *Plain Tales from the Hills.* Garden City: Doubleday, Page & Company, 1912.

—. *Rudyard Kipling's Verse, Inclusive Edition, 1885–1918.* Garden City: Doubleday, Page & Company, 1926.

—. *Jungle Books, The.* New York: Doubleday & Co., 1948.

Kipling Sites

NAULAKHA AND BATEMAN'S

Rudyard Kipling's homes, Naulakha in Dummerston, Vermont, and Bateman's in East Sussex, England, are owned, respectively, by The Landmark Trust USA and the National Trust, both dedicated to the conservation of historically important structures. Naulakha has been restored to appear as Kipling built it, and contains furniture and artifacts from his years there; it is available for rent, usually by the week. For information:

Landmark Trust
Shottesbrook, Maidenhead
Berkshire SL6 3SW
England

Bateman's and its contents were left by Carrie Kipling (who survived her husband by three years) to the National Trust for Places of Historic Interest or Natural Beauty, which manages the house as a Kipling museum, open to the public.

For information:
The National Trust
36 Queen Anne's Gate
London SWI H 9AS
England

Sources of Illustrations & Permissions

Front cover, 24, 34, 66, 81, 84, 96, 97, 104, 116: The Landmark Trust USA, Inc., Brattleboro, Vermont.

x, 31, 63, 76, 77, 79, 82, 87, 110, 119, 124, 164, 174, 177: Various sources including *A Ken of Kipling*, New Amsterdam Book Company, New York, 1899 and the Library of Congress, Washington, DC.

3, 4, 16: The photographic collection of the Rochester Historical Society, Rochester, New York.

37, 40, 42, 71, 72, 78, 103, 122, 152: Howard C. Rice Jr. Collection, Marlboro College, Marlboro, Vermont.

Excerpts from Rudyard Kipling works throughout and art on pages 31, 42, and 110 used by permission of A.P. Watt Ltd on behalf of The National Trust, London, England.

"In the Keddah" from the Kipling Manuscript Collection, Rice Library, Marlboro College, Marlboro, Vermont, used by permission.

Index

List of Kipling Works Quoted in Text

STUART MURRAY

Stuart Murray has been a book and magazine editor and a journalist for more than twenty-five years and has written ten novels and five works of nonfiction, including *Shaker Heritage Guidebook* (Golden Hill Press) and *Norman Rockwell at Home in Vermont, The Arlington Years, 1939-1953* (Images from the Past). Murray co-authored *Norman Rockwell's "Four Freedoms"*—co-published by Berkshire House and the Norman Rockwell Museum in Stockbridge—an alternate selection of the Literary Guild and recommended by the American Library Association.

In telling the little-known story of Rudyard Kipling's four years in America, Murray worked with the Howard C. Rice Collection at Marlboro College, and the holdings of The Landmark Trust at Naulakha, Kipling's former home in Dummerston, Vermont, and with numerous other archives.

Murray lives with his family in the Hudson Valley.

IMAGES FROM THE PAST

publishing history in ways that help people see it for themselves

OTHER BOOKS BY STUART MURRAY

NORMAN ROCKWELL AT HOME IN VERMONT
THE ARLINGTON YEARS, 1939–1953

The story of Norman Rockwell's dynamic years in the Vermont village where he painted some of his greatest works, including "The Four Freedoms" and "Saying Grace." Inspired by the "everyday life of my neighbors," the artist created storytelling pictures that have touched the hearts of millions around the world.

7" x 10"; 96 pages; 13 Rockwell paintings and sketches and 32 historical photographs
in black and white; index; regional map, list of area museums, selected bibliography
ISBN 1-884592-02-3 Paperback: $14.95

THE HONOR OF COMMAND
GENERAL BURGOYNE'S SARATOGA CAMPAIGN, JUNE–OCTOBER 1777

With the fate of the British Empire in the balance, the inexperienced Burgoyne led a powerful army of war-hardened veterans south from Canada to deal a fatal blow to the American Revolution. Hungering for "the honor of command" to advance his ambitious career, Burgoyne was doomed by his own shortcomings and the valor of the rebels he so fatally underestimated. The Saratoga Campaign from Burgoyne's perspective.

7" x 10"; 128 pages; numerous illustrations and maps; index; regional map,
listing of area historic sites, selected bibliography
ISBN 1-884592-03-1 Paperback: $14.95 Publication August 1997

Another Images from the Past title you might enjoy:

REMEMBERING GRANDMA MOSES
by Beth Moses Hickok

The story of a Christmastime visit in 1934, four years before Grandma Moses' "discovery," told in affectionate detail with excerpts from the author's diary and letters. Hickok, a first-time published author at 83, provides a direct link to the famous artist.

6" x 9"; 64 pages; portraits of Grandma Moses from 1947 and 1949,
9 historical photographs and 9 contemporary photographs in black and white
ISBN 1-884592-01-5 Paperback: $12.95

Available at your local bookstore or from Images from the Past, Inc.,
Box 137 Bennington, Vermont 05201 (888) 442-3204 Catalog available.
When ordering, please add $3.50 shipping and handling for the first book and
$1 for each additional. Add 5% sales tax for shipments to Vermont.